Cambodia and Kent State

Cambodia and Kent State

In the Aftermath of Nixon's Expansion

of the Vietnam War

James A. Tyner and Mindy Farmer

The Kent State University Press

Kent, Ohio

© 2020 by The Kent State University Press, Kent, Ohio 44242
All rights reserved
ISBN 978-1-60635-405-6
Manufactured in the United States of America

Cataloging information for this title is available at the Library of Congress.

Contents

Preface   vii

1 The Path to May 4 · 1

2 Cambodia after May 4 · 21

3 Kent State and Cambodia: Reconciliation · 49

Notes · 65

Preface

On Thursday, April 30, 1970, President Richard Nixon announced before a live television audience his controversial decision to attack enemy bases in neutral Cambodia. "We take this action," Nixon explained, "not for the purpose of expanding the war into Cambodia but for the purpose of ending the war in Vietnam and winning the just peace we all desire." Nixon's words and actions set into motion a complicated series of events with tragic consequences that would forever connect Cambodia and Kent State University.

For many antiwar activists in the United States, Nixon's explanation rang hollow. In their minds, Nixon's announcement seemed more like an expansion of the war than a way to achieve peace. Throughout the weekend, protests of the "Cambodian Incursion"—the preferred euphemism coined by the Nixon Administration for what was, by definition, an invasion—erupted on at least 132 college campuses. At Kent State University in Ohio, shortly after noon on Monday, May 4, 1970, thirteen seconds of rifle fire by a contingent of twenty-eight Ohio National Guardsmen left four students dead, one permanently paralyzed, and eight others wounded. The shootings solidified the national divide over America's involvement in the Vietnam War. In the month after the shootings, students organized protests and administrators across the country shut down campuses in what remains the largest student strike in the nation's history. Nixon described the aftermath as the "darkest days" of his presidency.

In Cambodia, President Nixon's announcement to attack enemy bases in Cambodia renewed the call for a government independent of Western power and influence, a call that, after many twists and turns, would result in civil war and the rise of the brutal Khmer Rouge. Following the invasion, Cambodia suffered a series of violent conflicts: five years of civil war and genocide.

Decades after the tragic events that unfolded on May 4, 1970, the cause of the protests has dimmed. Subsequent generations are vaguely aware that the shootings—often called the "Kent State Massacre" off campus but known as the "May 4 shootings" in Kent and northeast Ohio—happened within an era of antiwar protest at Kent State. Fewer Americans know that the triggering event of those spring protests was the expansion of the war into Cambodia. Even fewer are aware of the tragic history that unfolded in Cambodia following Nixon's decision. To facilitate better understanding of this piece of history, we detail here the decisions and events leading up to Nixon's announcement and the subsequent protests and violence at Kent State. We focus on Nixon's challenge of achieving "peace with honor" in the Vietnam War while battling discord at home, and we highlight the importance of the draft in spurring antiwar protests and examine Nixon's application of the "madman theory" in Vietnam to make his military choices seem unpredictable and vicious as he withdrew troops. We then move to document Cambodia's place in the broader Vietnam War. When students protested at Kent State and elsewhere, they did so with a belief that Nixon's decision to expand the war in order to attain peace was a fool's errand. Bombing campaigns and ground operations conducted on Cambodian territory, they argued, would only fan the flames of a regional conflagration. In retrospect, the premonitions of the protesters were tragically correct.

Effectively, we hope to provide some modicum of understanding of the events leading up to the tragic shootings at Kent State and of what happened afterward. Why did Nixon decide to invade Cambodia? How did Cambodia figure into the larger conflict in Vietnam? What happened in Cambodia after the invasion? We believe it is vitally important that future generations understand that alongside four deaths in Ohio, there were many hundreds of thousands of deaths in Cambodia.

The May 4 Memorial at Kent State University sits atop a grassy hill next to Taylor Hall. The site consists of four granite pylons with a walkway and a forty-eight-foot bench. Throughout autumn, oak trees wrap the memorial in curtains of vibrant orange, red, and yellow, while in springtime, daffodils spring forth, a testament to renewed hope and rebirth. Inscribed on the memorial are three words, asking visitors to "inquire," "learn," and "reflect." In this brief monograph, we take to heart this message, as we inquire, learn, and reflect upon the fate of Cambodia after Kent State. We imply no causality. However, the histories of these events remain conjoined, in that Nixon's decision affected the lives of not only countless Americans but also countless Cambodians.

We mourn the deaths of Allison Krause, Jeffrey Miller, Sandy Scheuer, and William Schroeder; and we grieve for millions of unnamed victims who perished in Cambodia in war and genocide. As we inquire into the tragedy made tangible on May 4, 1970, we want to learn from and reflect upon the past. As we remember the lives lost on that warm spring day in Kent, Ohio, we should remember also the tragedy that befell Cambodia after Nixon's decision. In so doing, we should remember also that the protests at Kent State University were not simply a call to end the expanding war in Southeast Asia; the protests also called for peace throughout the world.

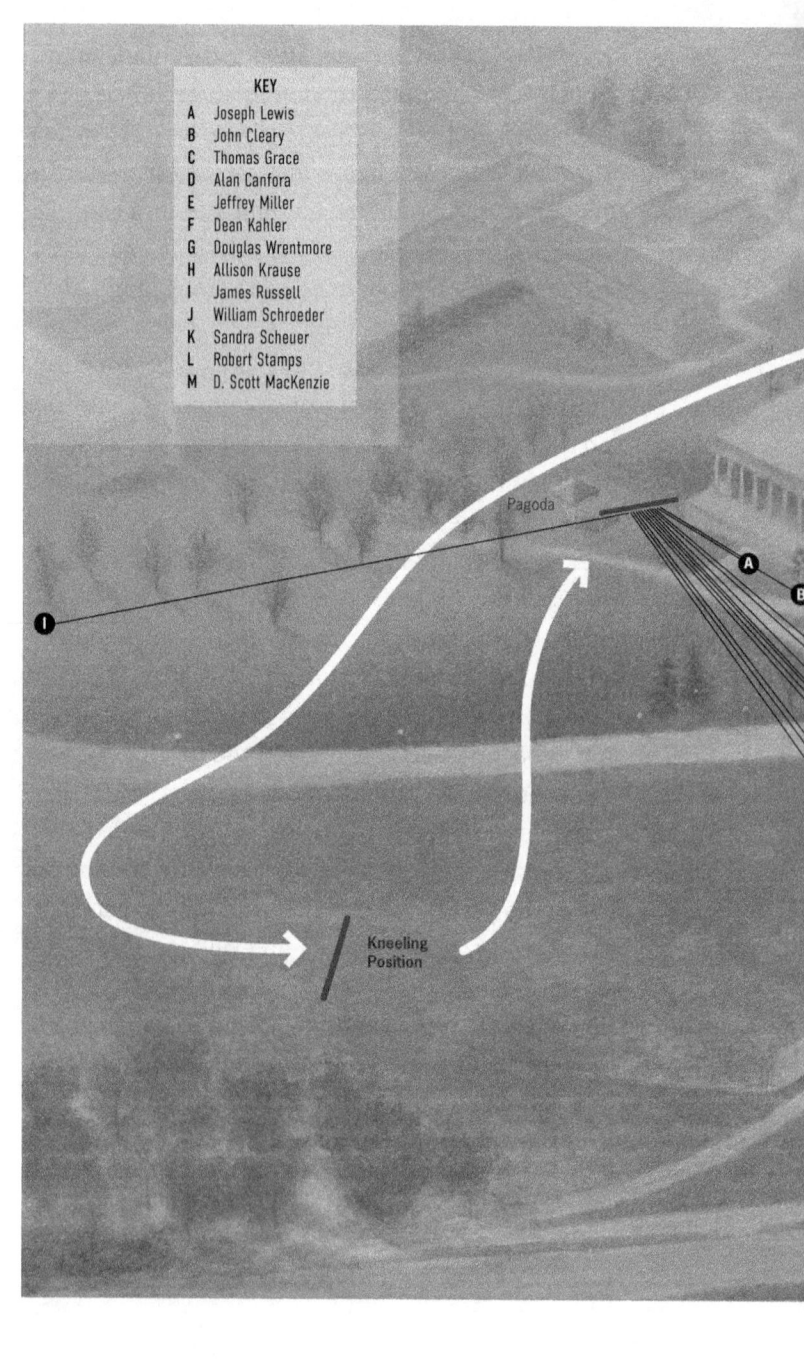

KEY

A Joseph Lewis
B John Cleary
C Thomas Grace
D Alan Canfora
E Jeffrey Miller
F Dean Kahler
G Douglas Wrentmore
H Allison Krause
I James Russell
J William Schroeder
K Sandra Scheuer
L Robert Stamps
M D. Scott MacKenzie

Pagoda

Kneeling
Position

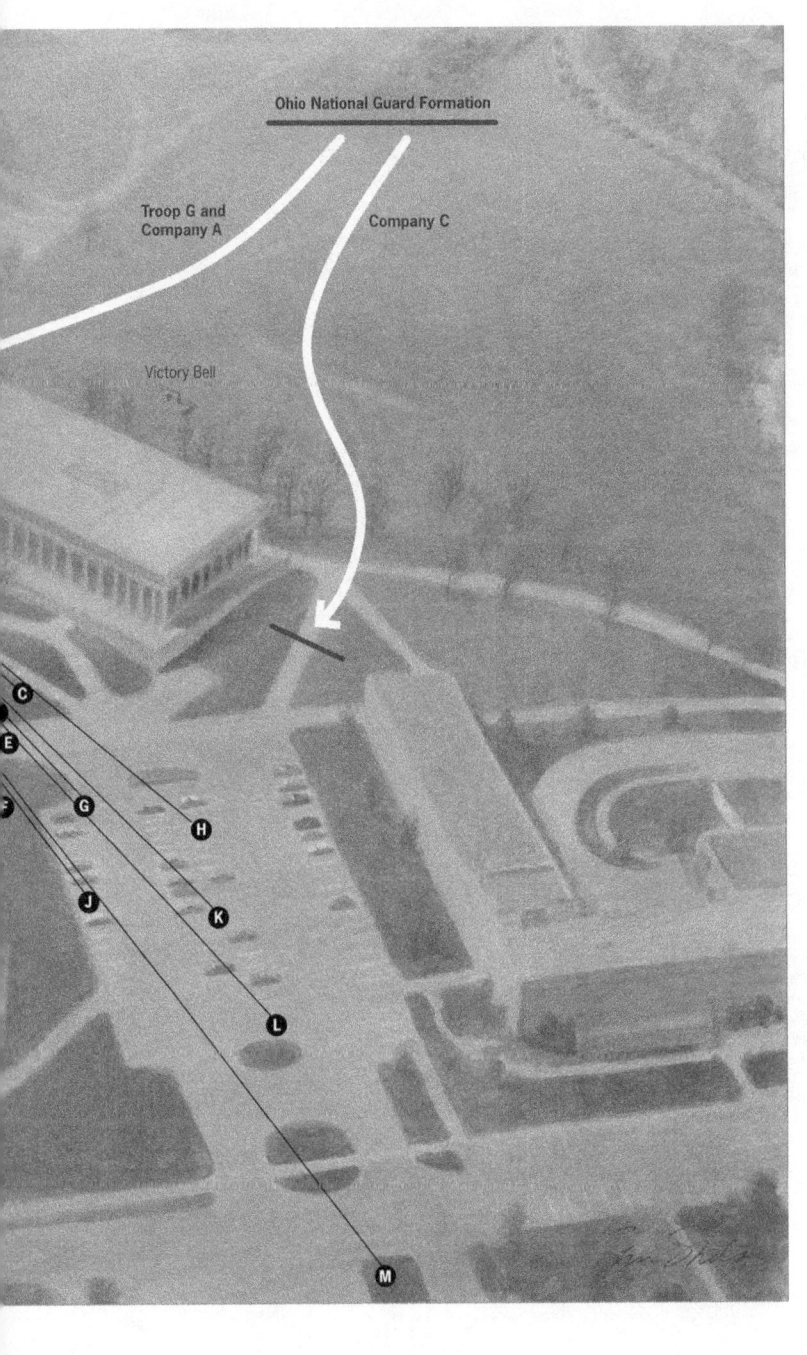

CHAPTER I

The Path to May 4

Many readers are aware of the events that transpired on May 4, 1970. The decision of President Richard Nixon to send US troops into Cambodia, and thereby enlarge the Vietnam War after previous statements of ending the war, sparked protests across the country. In Kent, Ohio, during a weekend of student-led demonstrations, Governor James A. Rhodes deployed the National Guard. On Monday, May 4, the demonstrations turned deadly. Sixty-seven shots rang out in just thirteen seconds. Two students died immediately, two would die later that day, one was paralyzed for life, and eight others were wounded. Thirteen lives: all irreversibly changed in thirteen seconds.

How are we to understand, and to learn from, the immediacy of May 4, 1970? A beginning point is to recognize that the student-led protests did not result only in response to Nixon's decision of April 30. Instead, the protests were part of a broader movement for social justice that captivated a generation of Americans who witnessed violence both home and abroad. The demonstrations at Kent State University, quite simply, emerged within an era of social protests and collective action.

The Era of Protests and Collective Action

There is much debate over the exact start of the modern Civil Rights Movement, the period when black citizens fought for the same rights as white citizens in the face of extreme segregation and discrimination. Some scholars argue that it began with the Supreme Court's 1954 decision in *Brown v. Board of Education,* overturning the legal doctrine of "separate but equal." With this monumental ruling, the highest court in the land turned decades of legal segregation on its head, giving momentum to the fight for equality. Others argue the movement started three years later when Rosa Parks refused to move to the "colored section" of the bus, inspiring the Montgomery Bus Boycott, the first of many large-scale protests led by Martin Luther King Jr. There is, however, no debate surrounding the movement's success in securing major national legislative victories. In the midst of nationwide protests and violent, bloody clashes, particularly in the South, President Lyndon B. Johnson signed the Civil Rights Act of 1964, outlawing discrimination based on race, color, sex, religion, and national origin. While this was a watershed law, it still fell short of curbing segregationists from legally preventing African Americans from voting. In response, Johnson signed the Voting Rights Act of 1965, which outlawed discrimination at the polls and upheld the rights guaranteed in the Fourteenth and Fifteenth Amendments to the Constitution. While these laws did not end racial discrimination, the Voting Rights Act and the Civil Rights Act were major victories for civil rights activists.

The success of the civil rights movement inspired other minority groups to fight for their own equality. Soon women, Native Americans, members of the LGBT community, and others launched their own fight for equal rights. At every turn, Kent State students joined in the battle for social change. On October 28, 1960, a group of African American students demanded service at the segregated Corner Bar in the heart of downtown Kent in the middle of the very busy Greek Week. The sit-in ended without incident when the local police ordered the bartenders to serve the students.[1] Shortly after the sit-in, Daniel Thompson joined the Freedom Riders, a diverse group of students who pushed to desegregate the Greyhound bus system in the South. He was jailed and beaten for his actions.[2] Four years later, following in the footsteps of the Free Speech Movement in Berkeley, California, where a massive student strike forced college adminis-trators to recognize all types of political organizations, the radical Young Socialist Alliance (YSA) petitioned Kent State University's student government for recognition. The group succeeded in spite of president Robert White's declaration that YSA was "distasteful to the overwhelming majority of us."[3] And, in 1968, women across campus purposely stayed out past their curfew to challenge a rule that required only women to be in their dorm rooms by a certain time—or face severe consequences. After nearly a yearlong legal battle, Kent State eliminated its gendered curfew.[4]

As women fought against sexist rules, African American students launched one of the best and proportionally largest examples of student collective action in Kent State history. In November 1968, Black United Students (BUS), the first black student organization in the United States, convinced nearly all of the four hundred African American students on campus to walk out in response to the uni-versity's controversial decision to punish or expel African American students for their role in preventing the Oakland Police Department from recruiting members on campus. At the time, the Oakland police were at the center of several controversies related to their treatment of the Black Panther Party—an organization founded in Oakland to protect African Americans from police brutality but whose mis-sion and membership would grow into a much broader platform. When the recruiters arrived, 150 African American students, coupled with members from the newly formed Kent branch of Students for a Democratic Society (SDS), occupied the area around the recruit-ers, blocking their access to the campus and, more importantly, the student body. The protestors remained until 7:00 P.M., even as the campus police threatened to arrest them all.[5]

As the university struggled with how to punish these protestors, BUS members demanded amnesty. Instead, the university threatened expulsion. As the situation escalated, black students executed a powerful protest. On November 16, African American students across campus gathered their belongings and walked out of class and off campus. Some went home while others attended makeshift classes in Akron, but all agreed to stay away until the university agreed not to punish a single person for their actions in the Oakland police protest. After only a matter of days, the university acquiesced and BUS and the students they represented returned.[6] No charges were filed.[7]

While demonstrating alongside BUS, members of SDS also focused on protesting the Vietnam War, the other major source of activism in the 1960s. Like many organizations, the goal of Students for a Democratic Society, a large network of students joined in opposition to war, was multifaceted. They opposed the nuclear arms race, racial disparities, and the complacency of the US political system among other things laid out in the Port Huron Statement—a political manifesto written in 1962 that detailed the shortcomings of US domestic and foreign policies. However, as the Vietnam War progressed and the mandatory draft resulted in the deaths of even more soldiers, antiwar activism increasingly stole their attention. Antiwar protests frequently appeared on and off campus as students, many of whom fought in the war or knew someone who did, petitioned their government for change. Understanding the Vietnam War and Richard Nixon's promise to disentangle the United States from the violent conflict is critical to understanding the events of May 4, 1970.

Richard Nixon and the Vietnam War

Much like the Civil Rights Movement, there is a debate over the beginning of the Vietnam War. Did it start when the United States first committed to help the struggling French forces under President Dwight D. Eisenhower? Did the death of the first US soldier during John F. Kennedy's administration mark the starting point? Or did the war officially start when Lyndon B. Johnson committed US ground forces in 1965? Even more recently, scholars such as Mark Atwood-Lawrence have pushed to extend the roots of the war back to the earliest period of imperialism.[8] What is clear is that the struggle in Vietnam spanned five presidencies and scarred a generation of Americans linked to a war they did not always understand and a style of guerrilla fighting that stood in stark contrast to the world's previous conflict, World War II. By the time of Nixon's campaign for president, the national sentiment was clearly turning against US involvement in the Vietnam War.

The year of Richard Nixon's presidential campaign was aptly called the "Year that Rocked the World."[9] Unrest was evident at every level, from the local to the international. Americans witnessed the assassinations of Martin Luther King Jr. and Democratic presidential candidate Robert Kennedy; Lyndon B. Johnson's shock announcement to forgo running for a second term as president to focus on peace negotiations; and violent, televised firefights that caused the veteran news anchor Walter Cronkite to call the Vietnam War a "stalemate." Around the world there were major protests over the rights of minorities and young people. At Kent State, 1968 was the year of the dorm protests against the curfew and the BUS walkout. It was a time of enormous social and political change.

In the midst of this turmoil, Richard Nixon positioned himself as the candidate of "law and order." In response to the protests, he promised to speak for the "silent Americans," whom he would later famously dub the "silent majority." He argued that for too long the cry of vocal demonstrators had overwhelmed the voices of law-abiding citizens. Instead, he would listen to the people at peace in their homes, not the ones shouting in the street.[10]

While pledging to restore peace domestically, Nixon promised a "victorious peace," later known as "peace with honor," in the

Vietnam War. Unlike President Johnson, Nixon considered international affairs his strength. During his terms as a US congressman,
senator, and vice president to Dwight D. Eisenhower, he had developed a reputation for staunch anti-Communism. Eisenhower
often dispatched Nixon overseas to meet with international leaders. By the end of his second term, Vice President Nixon had traveled more than any other vice president before him. Through
these experiences, he developed a philosophy of world affairs that
was distinct from previous administrations. Unlike the idealists
before him who believed that democracy had to be protected and
promoted at all costs, Nixon adopted a more flexible, pragmatic
approach to world events. While he opposed Communism, he was
willing to negotiate with Communists in order to further the in-
terests of the United States. Together with Henry Kissinger, his
powerful ally who would quickly rise through the White House
ranks to become secretary of state, he would call this philosophy
"realpolitik."

During the campaign, Richard Nixon was so confident in his
ability to bring about peace in the Vietnam War, he intervened in
President Johnson's secret peace negotiations. In what is known as
the Chennault Affair, then candidate Nixon sent a secret message
to the South Vietnamese through his friend and fundraiser Anna
Chennault, stating they would get a better deal if they waited to
negotiate with the Nixon Administration. Chennault, who was born
in China and the widow of the US Major General Claire Chennault,
who created the feared Flying Tiger squadron of World War II aces,
was, because of her connections throughout Asia, the perfect con-
duit for the message.[11] Although Kissinger claims that Nixon never
admitted to such illegal impropriety, recent archival evidence has
made what was once a rumor into a documented offense.[12]

Candidate Nixon's meddling had the intended effect on the 1968
campaign. Although Hubert Humphrey, the Democratic candidate
for president, tried to distance himself from President Johnson's
policy, the pause in the peace process sent many American voters

searching for a new game plan. It was a tight, bitter race, but Nixon edged out Humphrey.

As president, Nixon knew that he faced an enormous challenge in fulfilling his campaign promise to end the Vietnam War with a clear victory, or, at the very least, with something that did not resemble a clear loss. For Nixon, America's credibility was at stake. Any sign of weakness, either politically or militarily, would jeopardize Nixon's approach to the Vietnam War. However, if Nixon appeared to waver in his promise to end the war swiftly, he risked immediate and public backlash from the antiwar movement.

Such was Nixon's political paradox. In order to appease the antiwar movement, Nixon knew that he needed to start to withdraw troops. He also knew that publicly announcing his plans would only empower the enemy and place the United States in a weak position at the negotiating table. The North Vietnamese were well aware of the growing demand in the United States for a quick end to the war, and they could easily wait out the United States rather than accept unwelcome terms of a surrender or even a ceasefire. Emboldened by the president's dilemma, Hanoi launched a new, violent offensive in early March 1969, which resulted in the deaths of 453 US soldiers in a single week, more than double the average.[13] While Nixon and his advisers developed a plan to strengthen the South Vietnamese Army without US troops, later termed *Vietnamization*, Nixon and his team worked on a new, aggressive bombing campaign in neighboring Cambodia.

Cambodia had long presented a problem to the US military. Since 1951, Vietnamese Communists dictated the conditions of revolution inside Cambodia, and throughout this period the fledging Communists in Cambodia supported, albeit grudgingly, this state of affairs. By 1960, however, the situation was rapidly changing. In the United States–supported Republic of Vietnam (South Vietnam), Communist insurgents pressed the North for permission to wage armed rebellion. Up until now, the Communist leadership in the North had urged patience, for fear of drawing the United States into a protracted ground war. However, in 1960 the National Liberation Front (NLF, colloquially known as the "Viet Cong") was established. Its purpose was to engage in guerrilla activities, foment a general Communist revolution in the South, and contribute to the ultimate reunification of Vietnam. The Vietnamese strategy, however, was conditional upon continued access to Cambodia. As Vietnamese forces enlarged their military efforts, they established numerous transportation routes and bases throughout eastern Laos and especially eastern Cambodia. Known collectively as the "Ho Chi Minh Trail," these supply chains would prove invaluable both for NLF insurgent activities and for larger military campaigns conducted by the North Vietnamese Army (NVA). Access to Cambodia, though, was conditional upon Cambodian leader Norodom Sihanouk's assurance or, at the minimum, acceptance of neutrality, a position he held throughout the 1960s.

Throughout his long tenure, Sihanouk attempted a delicate balancing act: to remain neutral in the face of an ever-increasing war conducted on his eastern border. Pragmatically, Sihanouk tried to play both sides of the Cold War. In 1963, for example, he refused US aid, nationalized the import-export sector of the economy, and closed Cambodia's privately owned banks. He hoped these steps would induce stronger relations with China and the Soviet Union and, in the process, curtail the escalating war in Vietnam from expanding further into Cambodia. However, by severing relations with the United States, Sihanouk further crippled Cambodia's faltering economy. Neither China nor the Soviet Union was able or willing to invest substantial funds into Cambodia; consequently, Sihanouk had to make drastic reductions in defense spending, thereby incurring the ire of Cambodia's defense minister, Gen. Lon Nol, and the military establishment. Moreover, the nationalization of foreign trade encouraged the commercial elite to trade clandestinely with Communist insurgents in Vietnam.

Out of respect for Cambodia's difficult position and also out of fear of public outcry, the United States left these sanctuaries largely untouched.[14] However, even before taking office, Nixon asked his transition team to provide a precise report on the sanctuaries to determine if a policy change was in order. While many on Nixon's team opposed attacking without provocation, Kissinger supported it and arranged a breakfast meeting between top military officials to develop a preliminary proposal.[15]

Nixon mulled over the controversial plan as he prepared to leave for his inaugural tour of Europe. Initially he said no, perhaps worrying that if the plan leaked it would overwhelm the news of his overseas trip. However, as the North Vietnamese increased their deadly assaults, Nixon vacillated. Finally, on March 15, 1969, the president called Kissinger to commence the operation with the clear directive that "The order is not appealable."[16] The operation was executed with as much secrecy as the situation allowed. Even the State Department, which Kissinger was not yet a part of, was kept in the dark until well after the order was given and, at the same time, a series of phony records was created to throw any potential investigators off the scent. The secret, sober plan that would expand the Vietnam War into a neutral country and forever link the fates of Kent State and Cambodia was innocently named Operation Menu, with supporting attacks called Breakfast, Lunch, Snack, Supper, Dinner, and Dessert.[17]

Two days after Nixon's fateful call to Kissinger, sixty B-52 bombers took off from Vietnam en route to target the North Vietnamese supply lines along the Cambodian border. The initial intelligence cables gave every indication that the attacks were a success. As historian Richard Reeves writes in his classic book on the Nixon presidency, "At the next Cabinet meeting, two days later, the President flatly stated that the war would be over by the following year but said that the public line had to be that the outlook was very tough; that was a way to retain public support for the war during secret negotiations."[18] Nixon's optimism was quickly challenged. The war would outlast his presidency.

As the bombs fell in Cambodia, Nixon and Kissinger believed that the Soviet Union was funding and supporting Ho Chi Minh and the North Vietnamese. There would be no chance for "peace with honor" without a thaw in the Cold War between the United States and the Soviet Union. Less than a month after Nixon authorized Operation Menu, Kissinger proposed a bold plan to start to repair the United States' adversarial relationship with Moscow. Kissinger hoped to use his relationship with the Soviet ambassador to establish a secret backdoor line of communication between Washington and Moscow. In April 1969 Kissinger outlined his talking points to convince the Soviet Union to join in the conversation:

> The President has reviewed the Vietnam situation carefully.
>
> He will not be the first American President to lose a war, and he is not prepared to give in to public pressures which would have that practical consequence.
>
> The President has therefore decided that he will make one more effort to achieve a reasonable settlement. If it fails, other measures will be invoked.
>
> These measures could not help but involve wider risks. U.S.-Soviet relations are therefore at a crossroads.
>
> The President is eager to move into an era of conciliation with the Soviet Union on a broad front. As a sign of this, he is willing to send a high-level delegation to Moscow to agree with the Soviet Union on principles of strategic arms limitations. He is also willing to consider other meetings at even higher levels.[19]

Kissinger understood that the Soviet Union was no more likely to accept a defeat in the Vietnam War than the United States. However, he also knew that both countries were suffering from the enormously expensive arms race. By engaging in serious talks to limit nuclear weapons with the Soviets, Kissinger hoped the North Vietnamese would feel less confident in Soviet support as they approached the peace talks. This ambitious maneuver was an excellent example of the strategy of realpolitik in practice and the related but separate idea of détente. A French word meaning relaxed, détente described the Nixon administration's willingness to accept a period of eased world tensions in the midst of the Cold War rather than previous administrations' goal of uniting the world under democracy.

To buy time and public approval, Nixon announced the first of a series of troop withdrawals in the summer of 1969. Further, he capitalized on the success of Apollo 11 to launch a Pacific tour not so subtly highlighting the United States' unmatched engineering and technical expertise. While in Guam, Nixon informally outlined what would grow to become the Nixon Doctrine. The president explained that, while the United States would always honor its treaties and allies, it was time for the Asian nations to protect themselves. The United States would no longer intervene in every fight for democracy.[20] This was another drastic change from the typical Cold War mentality, and it set the stage for Vietnamization.

While the troop withdrawal was a welcome announcement for antiwar activists, it did little to turn the tide of protests. On October 15, 1969, Allison Krause, one of the victims of the May 4 shootings, marched front and center during the Kent State protest of the much larger national Moratorium March to End the War in Vietnam. The protest, one of the largest in Kent State history, snaked from the center of campus to downtown. The handful of war supporters was dwarfed by the long trail of students and like-minded supporters. Similar scenes were repeated across the country. The *Daily Kent Stater,* Kent State's student newspaper, captured the frustration: "Americans who have spent years writing futile letters to their congressmen and the president, who have joined antiwar organizations, who have voted for supposed peace-candidates, and who have expressed their antiwar sentiments to their friends are tired of being ignored. Today they are going into the streets to make their voices heard."[21] Exactly one month later, Krause traveled to Washington, DC, to join approximately five hundred thousand demonstrators in a major protest against the Vietnam War. It was another stark reminder of the nation's growing war weariness.

Even though troop withdrawals were important to the antiwar movement, they failed to address another major demand—the call for an end to the draft. While the draft had been in place since shortly before the United States entered World War II, the number of draftees tripled after President Johnson escalated the Vietnam War in 1965. As this number grew, so did the number of deferments. However, these deferments were inherently unequal. African Americans, other minorities, and poor white Americans were much more likely to be forced into service than their white middle-class counterparts. Originally, deferments were designed to drive talented men into areas of employment on par with military service, a theory known as "manpower channeling." Unfortunately, the majority of these jobs required either professional training or college degrees, both of which were financially out of reach for many American men. Even medical deferments favored the privileged. Private doctors conducted more thorough exams than the required military physicals. Consequently, draftees with a history of medical care had a higher chance of receiving a medical deferment than those who could not afford their own doctors.[22]

Just as he promised to end the war, Nixon promised to end the draft. In a compromise, Nixon canceled the calls for a draft in November and December 1969 and transitioned to a new, fairer lottery system, but the draft itself remained. Young people, like Allison Krause, who opposed the draft and the war, had little recourse but to protest. Most eighteen-, nineteen-, and twenty-year-olds could not vote until 1971, when the Twenty-Sixth Amendment lowered the voting age to eighteen. Aptly, "Old enough to fight, old enough to vote" was a key slogan in the push to pass the amendment.

It was clear by the spring of 1970 that both Nixon's secret plans to negotiate with the Soviets and the North Vietnamese and his public announcements to withdraw troops while training the South Vietnamese needed more time to be successful. In March, the focus once again turned to Cambodia when Prince Sihanouk was replaced in a coup by the pro-American leader Lon Nol. Eyeing

President Richard Nixon points to key areas of Cambodia during his address to the nation on April 30, 1970. (Courtesy of Richard Nixon Presidential Library and Museum, NLRN-WHPO-3448-21A.)

an opportunity for a major shift in the power dynamic, the Nixon administration quickly ordered aid, delivered through back channels, to help Lon Nol defeat his biggest source of opposition, the Communist Khmer Rouge. Despite fierce objections from his staff, Nixon also authorized one of his most controversial operations of the entire war, the Cambodian incursion. Initially, the Nixon administration hoped to keep the operation secret, but as the news of a potential invasion started to leak, the president scheduled an address to the nation for Thursday night, April 30, to speak to the public directly. On paper, the plan seemed simple—send thirty thousand US soldiers and fifty thousand South Vietnamese soldiers across the Cambodian border to destroy Communist bases from the ground—but the domestic reaction proved much more complex than the Nixon administration imagined.[23]

The May 4 Shootings

As many in Nixon's circle feared, President Nixon's Cambodia address was met with immediate protests. At Kent State, a group of history students—some of whom were Vietnam veterans and who called themselves World Historians Opposed to Racism and Exploitation (WHORE)—distributed leaflets on campus, encouraging students to meet at noon at the Victory Bell on Friday, May 1. In front of a crowd of about three hundred students, WHORE symbolically buried a copy of the US Constitution that one of the organizers ripped from his history textbook. The group also called for another, more organized protest at noon on Monday, May 4, 1970. A few hours later, another three hundred students gathered in support of BUS and in solidarity with the antiwar protests at Kent State and nearby Ohio State University.[24]

Once the White House learned of the protests, Nixon visited the Pentagon for a briefing on the new Cambodia actions. While there, he was greeted warmly by a group of employees. When one of them expressed her appreciation for the president's speech, Nixon responded with words that would haunt him:

> You see these bums, you know, blowing up the campuses. Listen, the boys that are on the college campuses today are the luckiest people in the world, going to the greatest universities, and here they are burning up the books, storming around about this issue. You name it. Get rid of the war there will be another one.[25]

That night, as most Friday nights, people from Portage County and the surrounding areas gathered in downtown Kent to drink, listen to local bands, and watch basketball with their friends. This night, however, was different. A group of students, some of whom had attended the earlier protests, started to chant against the war, while a local motorcycle gang, the Chosen Few, revved their engines and performed tricks in the street. The scene quickly grew more chaotic as unknown persons started small fires in the streets. As the situation escalated, the Kent mayor made a major mistake. He declared a state of emergency, closing the bars and sending a large group of drunk, dazed, and frustrated patrons into the streets alongside the protestors. As police officers fired tear gas, those in the crowd made their way to their homes, but not before vandalizing a number of downtown businesses.

Dismayed by the damage to the city and worried about the rumors that another more radical group was preparing to occupy the city, mayor LeRoy Satrom notified a liaison to governor James A. Rhodes that the National Guard, already in northeast Ohio in response to striking members of the Teamsters Union, should be put on alert in case the situation continued to escalate. Rhodes was behind in the polls in a tight race for the US Senate. As the law-and-order candidate, he was happy to oblige Satrom's request.[26]

The next morning started innocently, as some of the agitators from the night before went back downtown to help the business owners repair their damaged storefronts. But as night fell, the situation again grew tense. As a symbol of the military on campus, the headquarters of KSU's Reserve Officer Training Corps (ROTC) had long been a target of campus protests. Around 7:30 P.M. on Saturday, May 2, a group of around six hundred students and onlookers gathered around the Victory Bell. The crowd marched around campus, gathering supporters until the group swelled to between one thousand to two thousand people.[27] Just after 8:00 P.M., they shifted to the ROTC building where some in the crowd threw rocks and tried to set the beleaguered building on fire. After several more minutes, a small fire caught in the corner of the building and the fire department was called in to quell the blaze. When firefighters arrived at 9:00 P.M., protestors tried to cut their hoses and block them from the building.[28]

What happened next is the source of some of contention.[29] When the fire department first left the scene, the fire appeared to be out. However, shortly after the Kent State and Portage County police arrived to disperse the students, the blaze grew out of control. Members of the Ohio National Guard, having been placed on notice the previous evening, arrived at Kent State University around 10:00 P.M. as the wooden ROTC building burned to the ground.[30]

Even though the ROTC building was in poor condition and slated for demolition, the damage to university property was hard to overlook in the minds of many, including Governor Rhodes. On Sunday morning, just hours after his final debate, the Ohio governor arrived to tour the smoldering shell of the building. At a press conference downtown, he took a hard line against the students:

Last night I think that we have seen all forms of violence—the worst. And when they start taking over communities, this is when we're going to use every part of the law enforcement agencies of Ohio to drive them out of Kent. . . . They're worse than the "Brown Shirt" and the communist element and also the "night riders" in the vigilantes. They're the worst type of people that we harbor in America. And I want to say that they're not going to take over the campus.[31]

The governor's statement only inflamed an already tense situation. That night, students staged a sit-in in the middle of the main entrance to campus. They demanded to speak with the president of the university. At first, it seemed as though the Guardsmen would grant their wish, but instead the commanding officer ordered the group of students to disperse and, after a standoff, launched tear gas into the crowd. As they fled to their dorms, two students were wounded with bayonets.[32] The Guard acted under the belief that Governor Rhodes signed an edict banning all demonstrations. He had not. It was one of many communication breakdowns.[33]

The weather on May 4 was nearly idyllic, but there was clearly a storm brewing on campus. Due to the events of the weekend, the rally initially called for on May 1 became about so much more than just Nixon's announcement of the Cambodian Incursion. By noon, thousands of students, staff, and onlookers gathered at the

A crowd gathers in front of the burned ROTC building just before noon on May 4, 1970. (Photo by Frank Smith. Courtesy of Kent State University Libraries, Special Collections and Archives.)

Victory Bell as a line of National Guardsmen stood in formation across the Commons in front of the shell of the ROTC building. As the protesters hurled insults, the Guard responded with tear gas.[34]

Once again acting as though the rally had been banned, the general in command of the Guard ordered three of his units to advance on the crowd. The men split into two groups—one went right and one went left—to disperse the protestors. The main force of Troop G and Company A continued the maneuver until the troops reached the practice football field. With protesters directly in front of them, in one of the most iconic images from the day, members of the Guard kneeled and aimed at KSU student Alan Canfora as he waved a black flag. With their teargas canisters running low, the men regathered and appeared to march back toward their original formation in front of the burned-out ROTC building.[35]

The Ohio National Guard moves to disperse the crowd gathered around the Victory Bell. (Photo by Kent State University's News Service. Courtesy of Kent State University Libraries, Special Collections and Archives.)

People ducking and running for cover in the Prentice Hall parking lot where four students were shot and killed. (Photo by Kent State University's News Service. Courtesy of Kent State University Libraries, Special Collections and Archives.)

At approximately 12:24 P.M., Troop G and Company C reached the apex of a steep hill, known as Blanket Hill, near the Don Drumm sculpture and the Pagoda. Some protestors threw rocks at the Guard and some Guardsmen threw them back, but no rocks were thrown immediately prior to the shooting. While there is much debate over why so many Guardsmen turned and fired, the results of their actions are clear.[36] Their sixty-seven shots wounded nine students, ended the lives of four promising young adults—Allison Krause, Sandy Scheuer, Jeffrey Miller, and William Schroeder—and traumatized a school, city, and a nation. For this reason, we know May 4, 1970, as the "day the war came home."

Moments after the shooting, bystanders gather around injured student Joseph Lewis as the Ohio National Guard looks on. Both the Don Drumm sculpture and the Pagoda are visible. (Photo by Kent State University's News Service. Courtesy of Kent State University Libraries, Special Collections and Archives.)

CHAPTER 2

Cambodia after May 4

On May 4, 1970, the Vietnam War "came home" to Kent, Ohio. In Cambodia, ten thousand miles away, war had already taken up residence. When students at Kent State and other college campuses protested Nixon's decision to bomb Cambodia, thousands of men, women, and children had already died in the country. Sadly, for many other Cambodians, the "darkest days" were yet to come.

The shootings of May 4, 1970, occurred far from the Cambodian genocide, but the stories of both tragedies intertwine. While many readers may know that the protests at Kent State were related to the antiwar movement generally, few understand that Nixon's decision to invade Cambodia was the event that triggered the protests. Unfortunately, fewer still fully understand the context of Nixon's decision and the consequences for the people of Cambodia. In this chapter, we detail the rise of the Communist Party of Kampuchea (CPK), better known as the Khmer Rouge. For many historians, the Khmer Rouge regime constitutes one of the most brutal and oppressive periods of the twentieth century. Between April 17, 1975, and January 6, 1979, the CPK carried out a genocide in Democratic Kampuchea (as the Khmer Rouge renamed Cambodia), which is, in many respects, unparalleled.[1] The CPK—based on an eclectic understanding of Marx, Lenin, and Mao—embarked on a massive program of social engineering. In its attempt to remake Cambodia into a modern industrial state, the CPK launched a "Super Great Leap Forward" that included the mass collectivization of labor and communal eating, forced marriages, the destruction of urban areas, the abolition of private property and currency, and the prohibition of religion. These practices were not part of an overall comprehensive design; indeed, the Maoist-inspired "Super Great Leap Forward" suggests more design than was present. Nor, for that matter, were most proposed policies ever put into practice. Those policies that did materialize, however, led to the death of approximately two million people in just under four years.[2] The total number of deaths translates into one-fifth to one-quarter of Cambodia's pre-1975 population.

War Comes to Cambodia

The long-standing Franco-Viet Minh War (1946–54), culminating with the defeat of the French at Dien Bien Phu, and the subsequent Geneva Accords, left the future of Indochina in doubt. Most pressing was the decision to divide Vietnam into two political entities, the Communist-led Democratic Republic of Vietnam (DRV) in the North, and a United States–supported Republic of Vietnam in the South, with nationwide elections scheduled in two years. For many observers, the cessation of hostilities was but a respite as the region assumed greater importance in the rapidly expanding Cold War between the United States and the Soviet Union.

For most people living in Cambodia, however, the future looked promising. In the previous year, the Khmer monarch, Norodom Sihanouk, had embarked upon a "Royal Crusade" for independence. Making appearances in Paris, Washington, DC, and even Tokyo, Sihanouk argued that he alone could keep his country free from Communism. His direct efforts largely went for naught, but French authorities were compelled to grant independence to Cambodia on

November 9, 1953, in large part because they were preoccupied with deteriorating conditions in Vietnam. For many Khmer revolutionaries, conversely, the year brought uncertainty in purpose. Prior to this time, the Cambodian revolution was an ad hoc assortment of individuals and groups, all operating with different objectives and methods. Throughout the 1940s, for example, many Cambodians sought to liberate their country from French colonialism; following independence, most of these revolutionaries laid down their arms and returned to farming.[3] Others were disillusioned with the monarchy and desired to overthrow the long-standing prince, Norodom Sihanouk. Still others pursued a more radical form of politics; these men and women wanted not to simply replace the existing system of governance with their own politicians but desired instead to effect sweeping changes throughout the whole of society. This latter group included a man best known as Pol Pot.

At the Geneva Convention of 1954, the Vietnamese Communists proposed a temporary division at the thirteenth parallel, just north of Saigon, with elections scheduled in six months to determine national unity. The French countered with a boundary along the eighteenth parallel, south of Hanoi, with no elections. This, in effect, would create two sovereign states: the Democratic Republic of Vietnam (DRV) in the North and the State of Vietnam in the South. As a compromise, Soviet foreign minister Vyacheslav Molotov proposed a partition along the seventeenth parallel, just north of Hue, with elections rescheduled to take place in 1956. Vietnamese leaders were dismayed by this turn of events; anything short of a unified Vietnam was a failure. Representatives of the People's Republic of China, however, pressured the Vietnamese to accept the terms; from their vantage point, any stability on the Indochinese peninsula was preferable to the specter of heightened US military intervention.[4]

The acquiescence of China, Vietnam, and the Soviet Union was a devastating blow for many Khmer Communists, for this signaled the willingness of foreign powers to sacrifice Cambodia in pursuit of their own nationalist objectives. High-ranking officials throughout the Communist Bloc decided to postpone revolution in Cambodia until conditions in Vietnam warranted it. This meant that the Khmer Communists would have to forestall armed insurrection. For the Vietnamese, the intensifying struggle against the United States was most important and, from their perspective, it was critical that Cambodia remain neutral, at least in the short term, to prevent the United States from establishing a base of operations on Vietnam's western border. It was for this military reason that the Vietnamese pressured the Khmer Communists to support Sihanouk.[5] Consequently, Vietnamese Communists proposed a dual strategy for the Cambodians. On the one hand, Khmer revolutionaries formed a legitimate political party, the *Pracheachon,* and, on the other hand, the Communists pursued other more clandestine strategies. For this second approach, Khmer cadres would assume public positions as, for example, teachers or journalists while secretly recruiting new members. The Cambodian Communists' reaction to Vietnam's strategy varied, revealing deep fissures, both ideological and strategic. Some veteran leaders continued to accept Vietnam's logic and supported, to a degree, an alignment with Sihanouk. Members of the Pol Pot faction participated, also to a degree, with these tactics. However, their basic objectives and methods differed strongly, as they were adamantly opposed to Sihanouk and believed firmly in their mission to impose a Communist society.

Cold War geopolitics dramatically influenced the Communist revolution in Cambodia. Notable in this regard is the complex interplay of both the Soviet Union and the People's Republic of China. Indeed, it is important to recognize that members of the Communist Bloc did not always present a unified or homogenous counterpart to Western democracy. In fact, a fundamental clash in ideology and worldview often underscored the Sino-Soviet relationship.[6] Russian and Chinese Communists held very different understandings of both the nature of revolution and the path toward Communism. Indeed, as early as 1962, Moscow and Beijing criticized one another's perceived divergence from Marxism-Leninism.[7] For example, while both parties subscribed to a broad interpretation of Marxism-Leninism, in the Soviet Union Russian Marxists believed that revolution originates from the urban proletariat, whereas in China, Marxists believed that revolution comes from the rural peasantry.[8] Moreover, a number of Chinese Communists, unlike their Soviet counterparts, held a romantic view of the international Communist movement, that is, a worldwide Communist movement. These ideological differences reflect the different historical-geographical conditions of the respective countries and of the particular modifications made by Chinese and Russian Communists. Nevertheless, these fundamental differences of interpretation fomented deeper levels of mistrust that permeated other areas of concern, including class analysis, military strategy, and organizational structure.[9]

The growing rift between the Chinese Communists and Soviet Communists provides an important context to understanding events in Indochina, notably the actions by the Vietnamese Communists and, by extension, the actions of the Khmer Communists. Both China and the Soviet Union were global superpowers with substantial military forces. The armed forces of the DRV, conversely, relied on China and the Soviet Union. In turn, the guerrilla forces of the National Liberation Front (NLF; derisively known as the "Viet Cong") were dependent upon Hanoi. Interestingly, the Khmer Communists in theory could extend overtures to either the Vietnamese, Chinese, or Soviets. In practice, however, during the 1960s the Chinese and Soviets were willing to defer to Vietnamese objectives in their relationships with Khmer Rouge.

In June 1965, Pol Pot and a handful of Khmer Rouge cadres traveled to Hanoi. Their purpose was twofold: first, to undertake political studies and learn from Vietnamese military officials and, second, to discuss the role of the Khmer Communist movement.[10] By this point, US military involvement in Vietnam had increased substantially. Following the passage of the Gulf of Tonkin Resolution on August 7, 1964, US military forces conducted aerial bombing campaigns against the North. It is probable that Pol Pot expected support from his Vietnamese counterparts to make contingency plans for armed struggle in Cambodia against Sihanouk; at the very least, Pol Pot probably hoped to acquire weapons needed for revolution.[11] In the end, Pol Pot's expectations were unfulfilled, as the Vietnamese Communists continued to view a neutral Cambodia as necessary to their immediate and most pressing objective of national reunification. Le Duan, secretary-general of the Vietnamese Communists, for example, explained that the Khmer's strategy of "self-reliant struggle" was inappropriate and defeating; moreover, as a revolutionary party the Khmer Rouge were subordinate to the Vietnamese and thus were in no position to make such demands.[12] Le Duan "recommended that the Cambodians combine building revolutionary bases in the countryside through unarmed mass mobilization with continued infiltration of parliament and government, in order to position the Party to make a bid for power, perhaps through violence, once the Vietnamese had won the war."[13] Consequently, Hanoi stressed the need for continued access to sanctuaries within Cambodia as well as the ability to transport troops and supplies into southern Vietnam along the Ho Chi Minh Trail. In fact, the Vietnamese Communists had recently reached an agreement with Sihanouk that allowed the NLF access to Cambodian territory; in exchange, the Vietnamese pledged to honor all territorial borders at war's end.

Having failed in his attempt to secure the go-ahead for armed rebellion, Pol Pot and his entourage traveled to China. There, they met several high-ranking officials of the Chinese Communist Party, including Deng Xiaoping and Liu Shaoqi.[14] Similar to their Vietnamese counterparts, however, Chinese officials cautioned the Khmer Rouge to remain focused on the forest as opposed to the trees; that is, the Chinese also viewed Cambodia as an important piece in the grand scheme of geopolitics, but it was not the decisive piece. Rather, the Khmer Rouge should suppress their nationalist aspirations for international realpolitik. Strikes against Sihanouk would encourage the Americans to expand the war into Cambodia; and the Vietnamese sought to avoid this prospect, even if it meant delaying the revolution in Cambodia.

In hindsight, America's military strategy achieved what Pol Pot was unable to do: bring about armed conflict in Cambodia. Beginning in 1965, as Pol Pot pleaded with his Communist counterparts in Hanoi and Beijing, US officials approved the aerial bombing of Cambodia in an effort to disrupt the southern extension of the Ho Chi Minh Trail. In a matter of four years, the US military, under President Lyndon Johnson, conducted more than 2,500 sorties over Cambodia.[15] In response to the US bombing of South Vietnam, both the NLF and NVA increased their use of Cambodian territory as sanctuary and resupply and, in turn, US officials expanded their military operations into Cambodia. In 1967 military advisers initiated Operation Salem House (later renamed Daniel Boone) whereby teams of six to eight American and South Vietnamese soldiers entered Cambodia seeking tactical intelligence. Initially, missions were restricted, confined mostly to northeastern Cambodia; over time, the theater of operation expanded to include the entirety of the Cambodia-Vietnam border. By 1970 US forces had conducted over 550 covert missions throughout Cambodia, with an estimated 150,000 Cambodian citizens killed as "collateral damage."[16]

In 1969 the air campaign escalated dramatically as incoming president Richard Nixon approved Operation Menu. Throughout this campaign, American B-52 pilots flew more than 3,800 sorties and dropped more than 100,000 tons of bombs on the Cambodian countryside.[17] The objective ostensibly was to eliminate NLF and NVA sanctuaries inside Cambodia and to disrupt, if not destroy, the Ho Chi Minh Trail. In reality, Nixon sought a means to extricate the United States from a steadily worsening situation in

Vietnam. Nixon campaigned on a platform of ending the conflict; he had no plan, other than buying time to achieve an "honorable" withdrawal.

Until 1970, US military operations inside Cambodia were of a covert nature. Officials within the Johnson administration cautioned against widening the war overtly into neighboring Cambodia.[18] Nixon had no qualms. On April 30, Nixon informed the American public of a massive offensive into Cambodia against "the headquarters for the entire Communist military operation in South Vietnam."[19] Superficially, the so-called "incursion" was a joint operation conducted with forces of the Armed Forces of the Republic of Vietnam (ARVN); this was, however, a facade to minimize America's involvement. Code-named Operation Shoemaker, the invasion involved more than forty-four thousand ARVN and US troops and was concentrated along the Cambodia-Vietnam border. Nixon stressed that the United States undertook the operation not for expanding the war into Cambodia but for ending the war in Vietnam and winning the peace.[20] When asked about the invasion, Henry Kissinger, Nixon's national security adviser, explained, "We're not interested in Cambodia. We're only interested in it not being used as a base."[21] He added, "We're trying to shock the Soviets into calling a conference and we can't do this by appearing weak."[22]

For the men, women, and children living in Cambodia, Nixon's decision was fateful. To this point, the expanding war was limited mostly to the eastern border region of Cambodia. Now the launch of Operation Shoemaker transformed Cambodia into the center of a maelstrom.[23] Nixon followed the ground invasion with intensified aerial bombing. On December 9, 1970, the president telephoned Kissinger to demand an escalation of air attacks farther into Cambodia: "They have got to go in there and I mean really go in. . . . I want everything that can fly to go in there and crack the hell out of them. There is no limitation on mileage and there is no limitation on budget. Is that clear?"[24] Previously, American pilots were restricted in the conduct of missions: air strikes were limited to within thirty miles of the Vietnamese border, and B-52 drops were not to target sites within a kilometer of any village.[25] Immediately after receiving Nixon's call, Kissinger telephoned Gen. Alexander Haig to relay the orders: "He [Nixon] wants a massive bombing campaign in Cambodia. He doesn't want to hear anything. It's an order, it's to be done. Anything that flies on anything that moves. You got that?"[26]

The aerial bombardment of Cambodia between January 1971 and August 1973 was one of the most brutal and concentrated displays of firepower yet. During this period, American planes targeted over seventy-six thousand locations throughout Cambodia.[27] Bombing runs had become so prevalent that air traffic congestion became a major problem. At one point during the campaign, B-52 sorties were as high as eighty-one per day. Throughout the entirety of the war in Vietnam, conversely, the maximum had been sixty per day.[28] By the time the air campaign was halted in late 1973, US B-52s had dropped over 260,000 tons of bombs on Cambodia—a figure that does not include the tonnage dropped by other American fighter planes. Estimates of Cambodian casualties range from 150,000 to nearly 750,000.[29]

The air war did not bring victory to either Lon Nol's republic or to the United States. It did create a groundswell of support for the Khmer Rouge—a fact that was widely known but covered up by high-ranking US officials. On May 2, 1973, for example, the Central Intelligence Agency's director of operations provided details on a new recruiting drive launched by the CPK:

> They [the CPK] are using damage caused by B-52 strikes as the main theme of their propaganda. The cadre tell the people that the Government of Lon Nol has requested the airstrikes and is responsible for the damage and the "suffering of innocent villagers." . . . The only way to stop "the massive destruction of the country" is to . . . defeat Lon Nol and stop the bombing. This approach has resulted in the successful recruitment of a number of young men.[30]

With the onset of Operation Menu, Sihanouk's days in power were numbered. Opposition from both the left and the right formed a political vice from which Sihanouk was unable to extract himself. The end came quickly. While traveling in France, Sihanouk had entrusted his government to Lon Nol and his pro-Western deputy prime minister, Prince Sisowath Sirik Matak. In Sihanouk's absence, however, Lon Nol and Sirik Matak launched attacks on the Vietnamese Communist positions inside Cambodia, organized anti-Vietnamese demonstrations, and reestablished ties with various non-Communist groups. Sihanouk condemned these actions but could do little else. On March 18, 1970, the National Assembly voted 89 to 3 to depose Sihanouk.[31]

The coup d'état was a turning point. Initially, Chinese leaders sought to align themselves with the government of Lon Nol and Sirik Matak. Crucial to this strategy was the necessity of retaining Vietnamese access to bases in Cambodia. Thus, the Chinese were willing to postpone the Khmer Communist revolution in order to help the Vietnamese defeat the United States. This, too, was the immediate intention of the North Vietnamese. Refusing, however, to work with the Chinese, Lon Nol adopted a hardline anti-Vietnamese and anti-Communist position. In part, this reflected Lon Nol's own political leanings; but it also reflected his misreading of the international stage. Lon Nol believed, naively perhaps, the rhetoric of Nixon. He supported the expanded US military presence on Cambodian soil as well as the ongoing bombing campaigns and the presence of thousands of troops of the Army of the Republic of Vietnam. Lon Nol believed also in Nixon's promise that military and economic aid would be forthcoming.

The Soviet reaction to the coup was tepid. As historian Lien-Hang Nguyen writes, "The Soviets opted for an even more conservative stance toward Cambodia than the Chinese dual-track policy. In addition to maintaining relations with the Lon Nol regime, the Soviet Union joined other third-party nations calling for an international conference to restore order in Cambodia and to guarantee its neutrality in the Vietnamese-American war."[32] Reflecting a Cold War pragmatism, the Soviets wanted to avoid either a US- or a Chinese-controlled Cambodia.[33]

At this point, Sihanouk made a fateful decision. The Chinese Communists, rebuffed in their overture to Lon Nol, encouraged Sihanouk to align with the Khmer Rouge. With few options, Sihanouk capitulated. On March 23, 1970, Sihanouk, now residing in Beijing, announced the formation of the Royal Government of National Union of Kampuchea, more commonly known by its French acronym GRUNK (Gouvernement Royal d'Union Nationale du Kampuchea). GRUNK was composed of several high-ranking Communist leaders. Khieu Samphan, for example, held multiple titles, including deputy prime minister, minister of defense, and commander in chief of the GRUNK armed forces; Hou Yuon served as minister of cooperatives and minister of interior; and Hu Nim served as minister of propaganda.[34]

The apparent defection of Sihanouk to the Communist revolution proved decisive for the success of the Khmer Rouge. Already motivated by the ongoing US military onslaught, now thousands of men and women throughout Cambodia rallied to Sihanouk's cause to reclaim the government. One survivor recalls, "On the river many monasteries were destroyed by bombs. People in our village were furious with the Americans; they did not know why the Americans had bombed them. Seventy people from Chalong joined the fight against Lon Nol after the bombing."[35] Another remembers, "The town of Chantrea was destroyed by US bombs. . . . The people were angry with the US and that is why so many of them joined the Khmer Communists."[36] Whereas in 1969 Khmer Rouge forces perhaps approached 4,000 members, by 1972 they numbered in excess of 20,000. Indeed, some US officials estimated Khmer Rouge troop strength at between 30,000 and 50,000 or even an incredulous 150,000.[37] From 1973 onward, the CPK steadily, relentlessly "liberated" Cambodia and established base areas from which to operate. By 1974 only the national capital, Phnom Penh, and a handful of provincial capitals remained outside the orbit of Khmer Rouge control.

The Cambodian Genocide

When the Khmer Rouge achieved military victory on April 17, 1975, its political future was far from certain. With Sihanouk's fall, the Vietnam War, in the words of Arnold Isaac, "fell on his helpless country like a collapsing brick wall."[38] Sustained and indiscriminate bombing, combined with brutal fighting between Lon Nol's troops, the Vietnamese Communists, and the Khmer Rouge exacted a horrifying toll on Cambodia's population, engendering a new expression: "The land is broken."[39] By war's end, approximately one-third of the country's bridges were ruined, two-fifths of the road network was unusable, and the railroad system was inoperable. Much of the country's productive infrastructure, including its lone oil refinery, had stopped working. Only 300 of 1,400 rice mills and 60 of 240 sawmills were functioning; and both timber and rubber production—Cambodia's major prewar commercial products other than rice—had declined to only one-fifth of prewar production levels. Moreover, upward of half of Cambodia's livestock was dead, killed from either fighting or bombing or used as food for the starving people.[40]

When the Khmer Rouge stood victorious on the streets of Phnom Penh in April 1975, they constituted neither a centralized, efficient political party nor a military force.[41] Their victory was the haphazard byproduct of the culmination of a series of concurrent revolutions, armed conflicts, and geopolitical machinations.[42] High-ranking members of the CPK understood that they did not enjoy popular support. In part, this was the direct outcome of their revolutionary strategy. As a Marxist-Leninist Party, secrecy was paramount for members of the CPK. Indeed, throughout the long years of revolution, both the party and its platform remained shrouded in mystery. In fact, so cautious was the CPK in its openness that it was not until 1977 that the CPK's existence and Pol Pot's leadership was publically acknowledged.[43] Moreover, most men and women who joined the Khmer Rouge did so in response to armed conflict and the sustained US-led bombing campaign that devastated Cambodia. Others joined in support of the ousted former monarch, Norodom Sihanouk. Very few soldiers of the Khmer Rouge were ideologically motivated.

These factors posed two immediate obstacles to subsequent forms of governance initiated by the CPK, the resolution of which would have considerable repercussions throughout the country. On the one hand, leaders of the Khmer Rouge were impelled to further disseminate, albeit guardedly, their overall political-economic objectives. To this end, political training sessions were cursory at best, with Communist ideology presented in simple terms. On the other, Pol Pot and other senior leaders determined that a strong central authority remained necessary, until the masses had elevated themselves to the appropriate level of political consciousness. In practice, this meant that high-ranking members of the CPK expressed considerable mistrust toward the people they ruled.

As specified in the Party Statutes of 1976, all party members must "be good and clean and be pure politically, ideologically, and organizationally."[44] In theory, all citizens over the age of eighteen were eligible to become party members; in practice, CPK leaders imposed strict qualifications. Prospective party members, for example, "must have had good and constantly combative activities, tested in successive revolution work in the unions, in the cooperatives, and in the Revolutionary Army" and "must have good and clean life morals and be good and clean politically."[45] Consequently, new recruits were required to complete an eleven-page biographical

Khmer Rouge soldiers eating in a communal dining hall. (Courtesy of Tuol Sleng Genocide Museum.)

form. Most of the thirty-two questions addressed information about the applicant's family members; questions of political activities and social networks were paramount.[46]

More broadly, the Khmer Rouge divided Cambodia's population into two main groups: "base" people and "new" people. The former class included men, women, and children who lived in rural areas that were liberated by the Khmer Rouge prior to April 1975. New people, also known as "April 17" people, included all those who were not Khmer Rouge cadres, party members, or base people. New people were almost exclusively urban in origin. Base people were classified as full-rights people, meaning that they were allowed to vote and serve in positions of authority. New people, conversely, were largely excluded from any political position, had fewer rights, and were subject to brutal treatment.[47]

To govern the country, CPK leaders promoted, rhetorically, a form of government known as democratic centralism. Based primarily on the writings of the Soviet Marxist Vladimir Lenin, democratic centralism combined democracy and centralism into a principle of political organization whereby workers, not state administrators, would be responsible for production decisions. Over time, democratic centralism acquired different meanings, as other Communist parties, including those in China and Vietnam, adopted the concept. In his speech of September 1977 Pol Pot explains, "We have solidly laid the foundations of our collectivist socialism, and we are continually improving them, while consolidating and developing them."[48] He continues: "We promote broad democracy among the

Khmer Rouge cadre attending a political education session. (Courtesy of Tuol Sleng Genocide Museum.)

people by a correct application of democratic centralism, so that this immense force will mobilize enthusiastically and rapidly for socialist revolution and construction, at great leaps and bounds forward."[49] In practice, the party leadership never relinquished ultimate authority over political, economic, or social programs.[50]

In the CPK's Four-Year Plan (1977–80) two primary objectives were identified: "to aim to serve the people's livelihood, and to raise the people's standard of living quickly, both in terms of supplies and in terms of other material goods" and "to seek, gather, save, and increase capital from agriculture, aiming to rapidly expand our agriculture, our industry, and our defenses rapidly."[51] These objectives were not mutually exclusive. Agricultural growth would produce the capital that would form the basis for eventual industrial self-sufficiency. The crucial component was to exchange agricultural surpluses for foreign capital.

CPK officials based their economic policies on principles established by the Non-Aligned Movement. During the 1950s and 1960s, many former colonies embarked on a particular economic strategy known as import-substitution industrialization (ISI). Proponents of ISI argued that lesser-developed countries should initially substitute domestic production of previously imported, simple consumer goods and then substitute through domestic production for a wider range of more sophisticated manufactured items.[52] Revenue saved from not having to import these goods could then be used to purchase other manufactured commodities that could not be produced given the country's overall level of industrial development. Such an approach is readily apparent in CPK documents. For example, minutes from a meeting held on May 8, 1976, state: "We will decrease importing items next year, including cotton and jute, because we are working hard to produce ours. We will import only some important items such as chemical fertilizer, plastic, acid, iron factory, and other raw materials."[53] This strategy was deemed most appropriate, as solutions were not to be found "by taking loans from the West or

Eastern Europe," for in so doing the CPK would lose their "self-reliant stance."[54]

Operating within an overall policy of ISI, the CPK identified items that their workers could effectively produce, both for domestic consumption and for foreign trade. On the home front, plans called for the promotion of items necessary to facilitate people's livelihoods: plates, pots, spoons, mosquito nets, shovels, hoes, and so on. In practice, most of these industries never materialized, although textile factories and some machine shops were in operation. Surviving documents indicate that the CPK was receptive to any number of imported goods but that economic efficiencies would be the determining factor in deciding the conditions of foreign trade. In a report prepared in 1976, a senior official explains, "We can export and sell many products such as kapok, shrimp, squid, elephant fish, and

Cambodian children prepare to work in the fields. (Courtesy of Tuol Sleng Genocide Museum.)

turtles. All of these products can earn foreign exchange. There are great possibilities for exporting peanuts, wheat, corn, sesame, and beans. The objective would be to save up these products for export. Almost anything can be exported, so long as we don't consume it ourselves, but set it aside."[55] The report further details, "We have the potential to achieve full quotas in rubber, cement, railroads and salt. We have progressed nicely, almost with empty hands. We have achieved good results. But the possibilities are even greater. We must expand the Plan. Our line is to stress industry and the working class as the basis."[56]

For senior members of the CPK, agriculture was determined to be the country's comparative advantage. According to the Four-Year Plan, "We stand on agriculture as the basis, so as to collect agricultural capital with which to strengthen and expand industry." And among the possible agricultural crops that could be pursued, rice was preeminent. To this end, Pol Pot declared in August 1976: "We have greater resources than other countries in terms of rice fields. Furthermore, the strength of our rice fields is that we have more of them than others do. The strength of our agriculture is greater than that of other countries in this respect. . . . It is the Party's wish to transform agriculture from a backward type to a modern type in ten to fifteen years. A long-term strategy must be worked out. We are working on a Four-Year Plan in order to set off in the direction of achieving this 10–15 year target."[57] To meet these objectives, CPK leadership determined that not only did the amount of land under rice cultivation need to expand; overall rice productivity was to triple to a national average yield of three tons per hectare per year. Thus, the CPK initiated a pragmatic course of action based on capitalist principles. From a competitive standpoint, rice was the obvious choice: "For 100,000 tons of milled rice, we would get $20 million; if we had 500,000 tons we'd get $100 million. . . . We must increase rice production in order to obtain capital. Other products, which are only complementary[,] will be increased in the future."[58]

A mobile work brigade excavating a canal for one of the many irrigation projects initiated under the Khmer Rouge government. (Courtesy
of Tuol Sleng Genocide Museum.)

For the CPK, an overriding difficulty associated with increased
rice production was the problem of water. According to the Four-
Year Plan, it was necessary to "increase the degree of mastery over
the water problem from one year to another until it reaches 100
percent by 1980 for first-class rice land and reaches 40–50% for
ordinary rice land."[59] Following a table of calculations indicating
the annual percentage increase projected between 1977 and 1980,
the text continues: "In order to gain mastery over water there must
be a network of dikes and canals as the basis. There must also be
canals, reservoirs, and irrigation pumps stationed in accordance
with our strategy."[60] The rapid and massive development of irrigation was crucial, necessitating the completion of over seven
thousand kilometers of dikes, dams, and canals and the construction of approximately 350 reservoirs.[61]

Under Khmer Rouge rule, forced laborers excavated thousands of kilometers of canals, with many workers dying in the process. (Courtesy of
Tuol Sleng Genocide Museum.)

Alongside the expansion of agriculture and irrigation systems,
senior officials of the CPK imposed a system of food rations. Workers were classified as either *kemlang ping* (full strength) or *kemlang
ksaoy* (weak strength), with the former consisting mostly of adults
and the latter consisting of small children and the elderly. Those
designated as full strength were further classified into two sub-
groups: kemlang 1, which consisted of young, able-bodied single
men and women working in mobile brigades; and kemlang 2, which
included married, able-bodied men and women who were divided
by sex but generally worked closer to the village. These work teams
were segregated by sex; males belonged to *kong boroh* and females

to *kong neary*. These brigades were set to work primarily on land clearance—digging canals and reservoirs and constructing dams and dykes. Kemlang 2 workers generally worked closer to their villages, performing such tasks as local woodcutting (for building materials or fuel), preparing and cultivating agricultural fields, and maintaining irrigation schemes. Lastly, the "weak strength" laborers (kemlang 3) engaged in lighter tasks.

Elderly workers were grouped into work teams known as *senah chun*, with male groups termed *senah chun boroh* and female groups *senah chun neary*. Duties for members of *senah chun* included sewing, gardening, collecting wood, and caring for children. Depending on the conditions and the attitudes of local Khmer Rouge cadres, some elderly workers might be required to labor in the rice fields or engage in other more strenuous work. Children under fourteen were assigned to work groups known as *kong komar*, with boys and girls separated into *kong komara* and *kong khomarei*, respectively. Children were responsible for watching after cows and water buffalo, light digging in gardens and fields, collecting firewood, and gathering cow dung for fertilizer.[62] Under the Khmer Rouge, consequently, food rations were, in theory, allocated based on the scale and scope of work performed. Workers who performed the heaviest manual labor were to receive the highest rations; those who engaged in the lightest tasks, as well as the elderly and the sick, received the smallest rations. Pregnant women or women who had just given birth, in theory, also received higher rations. In practice, very few people had adequate food or other necessities, with the so-called "new" people suffering most.

The new political economy of Democratic Kampuchea placed the majority of the population between the teeth of two powerful forces: on the one hand, a demand for surplus rice and agricultural inputs that justified severe labor policies and, on the other, an austere rationing system that subjected men, women, and children to starvation wages. These economic policies contributed, subsequently, to the direct violence that permeated Democratic Kampuchea.

Draconian economic policies, coupled with the fragility of CPK rule, impelled the development of a massive security apparatus designed to seek out and "smash" perceived external and internal enemies. First, Khmer Rouge cadres identified, arrested, and often killed former soldiers and officials of the previous governmental regime. Likewise, Vietnamese soldiers and "spies" were to be eliminated. Second, many high-ranking officials of the CPK cautioned against the presence of "internal" enemies, such as traitors and saboteurs. "New" people, by definition, were immediately suspect; more pernicious, however, were the so-called traitors among the ranks of the Khmer Rouge: disloyal soldiers, treasonous officials, and those cadres harboring "revisionist" or "bourgeois" tendencies.

It was the hurried implementation and resulting inefficiency of economic policies that led to widespread paranoia among the highest echelons of the CPK. Surviving CPK documents describe people arrested for "stealing" food or merely complaining about insufficient rations. Such punishment extended beyond the masses: CPK leaders also purged local officials who admitted that starvation was occurring in their areas. As the food crisis increased, the CPK blamed traitorous and inept low-level cadres of undermining the food production system. Thus, beginning in 1976, and intensifying throughout 1977, Pol Pot and his close associates initiated a series of purges against suspected traitors and reactionary elements within the party, as Khmer Rouge soldiers arrested, detained, and executed high-ranking cadres. Prior to their death, they were tortured and forced to confess their knowledge of and involvement in traitorous activities and to divulge the names of others. These "strings of traitors" would subsequently lead to more and more purges. In time, the Khmer Rouge arrested and executed en masse entire divisions and work groups.

On September 27, 1977, Pol Pot delivered a long-winded speech broadcast throughout Democratic Kampuchea.[63] This particular speech is meaningful, in part, because it expresses the official objectives of the Khmer Rouge. A recurrent theme throughout the

1977 speech, but prevalent also in scores of other public pronounce-ments and propaganda materials disseminated by the CPK, is that of defending the country. Pol Pot commanded his audience that the duty ahead was "to contribute to the national defense, the building up of the country, and the raising of the people's living standard, all toward carrying out, with a high sense of revolution responsibility, the glorious task which the Party has entrusted to them."[64] Pol Pot concluded that in the two years following their victory in 1975, the CPK had "successfully protected, strengthened and expanded the fruits of the revolution, the state power of the revolution, and totally safeguarded the independence, sovereignty, territorial integrity and borders of [Democratic Kampuchea] by relying on principles of complete independence, initiative and self-reliance."[65] Here, Pol Pot intimates that the Khmer Revolution was unique; that unlike all previous Communist revolutions, the Khmer Rouge achieved victory on their own. Not surprisingly, Pol Pot was remiss in his comments, for the Cambodian genocide was very much a product of Cold War geopolitics.

The Cambodian Genocide and America's Role

The standard narrative of the Vietnam War pits the United States and its allies against the Communist Bloc, notably China and the Soviet Union. After World War II, numerous presidential administra-tions increased US military presence in Southeast Asia in an effort to prevent the region from falling to Communism. This narrative, however, creates the false impression of a clear division between the democratic, capitalist West and the Communist, totalitarian East. In reality, US policy makers realized that the Communist Bloc was not monolithic and that it might be possible to drive a wedge between competing Communist factions. As it became clear that North Vietnam would emerge victorious, US strategists looked to stem the anticipated tide of revolution and contain "Vietnamese"

Communism to Vietnam. To this end, the Nixon administration began to extend covert support to China and, incredibly, the Khmer Rouge, looking to capitalize on both groups' historical animosity toward the Vietnamese.

As the Khmer Rouge solidified their rule over Cambodia, US officials made several diplomatic forays to encourage Chinese involvement in Cambodia and solicit cooperation from other Southeast Asian neighbors in an effort to isolate Vietnam. On November 26, 1975, Chatchai Chunhawan, the foreign minister of Thailand, met in Washington, DC, with US secretary of state Henry Kissinger and assistant secretary for East Asian and Pacific Affairs Philip Habib.[66] During the course of their conversation, Kissinger asked about Chatchai's recent meeting with Ieng Sary, one of the founders of the Khmer Rouge and a leader of the CPK:

KISSINGER: What is the Cambodian attitude?

CHATCHAI: The Cambodians want salt and fish. They wanted to barter for these items.

KISSINGER: Did Ieng Sary impress you?

CHATCHAI: He is a nice, quiet man.

KISSINGER: How many people did he kill? Tens of thousands?

HABIB: Nice and quietly!

CHATCHAI: Not more than 10,000. That's why they need food. If they had killed everyone, they would not need salt and fish. All the bridges in Cambodia were destroyed. There was no transportation, no gas. That's why they had to chase people away from the capital.

KISSINGER: But why with only two hours' notice?[67]

CHATCHAI: (Shrugs)

KISSINGER: What do the Cambodians think of the United States? You should tell them that we bear no hostility towards them. We would like them to be independent as a counterweight to North Vietnam.

CHATCHAI: Are you a member of the Domino Club?[68]

KISSINGER: I am.

CHATCHAI: The outer, most exposed belt of dominos is Cambodia and Laos. Thailand is in the inner belt and is less exposed.

KISSINGER: We would prefer to have Laos and Cambodia aligned with China rather than with North Vietnam. We would try to encourage this if that is what you want.

CHATCHAI: Yes, we would like you to do that. . . . The right wing is what we really have to worry about, not the left. The Chinese are 100 percent in support of Cambodia's being friends with Thailand.

KISSINGER: We don't mind Chinese influence in Cambodia to balance North Vietnam. As I told the Chinese when we last met when we were discussing the Vietnamese victory in Indochina, it is possible to have an ideological victory which is a geopolitical defeat. The Chinese did not disagree with me. . . . It is important that we [the United States] still have a presence in Southeast Asia. . . . I am, personally, embarrassed by the Vietnam War. I believe that if you go to war, you go to win and not to lose with moderation. We are aware that the biggest threat in Southeast Asia at the present time is North Vietnam. Our strategy is to get the Chinese into Laos and Cambodia as a barrier to the Vietnamese.

CHATCHAI: I asked the Chinese to take over in Laos. They mentioned that they had a road building team in northern Laos.

KISSINGER: We would support this. You should also tell the Cambodians that we will be friends with them. They are murderous thugs, but we won't let that stand in our way. We are prepared to improve relations with them. Tell them the latter part, but don't tell them what I said before.

Kissinger also agreed that China could—and should—have a free hand in both Laos and Cambodia. In practice, the assistance provided by China to the Khmer Rouge included facilitating trade in industrial and agricultural inputs, sending engineers to assist with various large infrastructural projects, and providing technical and scientific expertise.[69] Indeed, without assistance from China and

Southeast Asian neighbors, it is not clear that the CPK could have maintained an operational state apparatus, let alone consolidate its control over a country still reeling from years of civil war. Most notably, Kissinger approved and encouraged this critical assistance, despite knowledge that tens of thousands had already died.

In December 1975, US president Gerald Ford and Kissinger met with Indonesian president Suharto.[70] Ford explained that despite the "severe setback of Vietnam," the United States intended to maintain a "strong interest in and influence in the Pacific," notably Southeast Asia. Ford clarified, though, that the United States did not have any "territorial ambitions" in the region. Suharto inquired about China's aims, since Ford had just returned from a meeting in China. Both Kissinger and Ford assured Suharto that China did "not have expansionist aims." Conversation next turned to Vietnam. Ford acknowledged that the unification of Vietnam arrived sooner than expected and that there was concern over the possible influence of Vietnam on Laos and Cambodia. For Suharto, the prospect of an alliance between these three states was of considerable concern. Ford noted that there was "resistance in Cambodia to the influence of Hanoi" and that the United States was "willing to move slowly in . . . relations with Cambodia." Here, Ford's position echoed Kissinger's remarks one month earlier to the Thai foreign minister. Ford explained that the United States considered "the Cambodian government [the Khmer Rouge] very difficult" and yet, they afforded an opportunity to minimize Vietnamese influence.[71] Kissinger concurred, explaining, "We don't like Cambodia, for the government in many ways is worse than Vietnam, but we would like it to be independent." Kissinger reiterated, "We don't discourage Thailand or China from drawing closer to Cambodia."

If eight years of US aerial bombardment and military incursion during the Vietnam War helped bring the Khmer Rouge to power, subsequent diplomacy between US officials and Cambodia's neighbors solidified the control of the CPK and facilitated the Khmer Rouge in the implementation of their economic policies. By 1979 these policies had brought about the deaths of millions from disease, starvation, exposure, and execution. Most troubling is the fact that US administrations had knowledge of these atrocities as they were occurring. In 1976 the Ford administration allowed limited humanitarian assistance to the Khmer Rouge, including $50,000 in malaria medicines.[72] In 1977 the US embassy in Thailand sent a telegram to Washington, DC, clarifying the horrific conditions throughout Democratic Kampuchea.[73] According to this report, declassified only in 2009, US intelligence officers in the region were well aware of various resistance movements working to overthrow the Khmer Rouge. These resistance fighters, however, were "desperately short of funds, medicines, and ammunition." Indeed, so dire was the situation that "without foreign support" they were "struggling more for their own survival than actively resisting Khmer Rouge rule in Cambodia." Moreover, resistance leaders "described rising [death] tolls from disease, malnutrition and famine." They estimated that "the population of Cambodia may have been reduced by more than half."[74] According to the telegram, Chinese military personnel, stationed mostly in southern Cambodia, supported the CPK. The report goes on to acknowledge reports of ongoing purges by the CPK, including the executions of senior Khmer Rouge cadres such as Hu Nim and Hou Youn. The report's dire assessment continues:

Although the Khmer Rouge continue to seek to identify and eliminate anyone associated with the former regime, famine and disease have become the greatest threat to life in Cambodia. Malnutrition, malaria, intestinal disease, and now beriberi are reducing the population. Starvation is taking a greater toll, a fact which informants found damnable since they said Cambodia's rice harvest earlier this year was good. Interlocutors said that production had been sufficient to feed all Cambodians but [the CPK] is stock-piling rice and exporting even more, presumably to China, to satisfy trade import requirements. Sources calculate that 41,000 Cambodians have died in Koh Kong and Pursat Provinces. They commented that it was not uncommon for half the population of a village to have perished. Both interlocutors estimated that there are only three million of the former seven million Cambodians still alive. The fruit of the Khmer Rouge rule might well be the extinction of the Cambodian race, in their assessment.[75]

At this time, it is not clear what reaction this assessment generated within the Carter administration. However, the document makes it obvious that US officials were aware of conditions on the ground in Democratic Kampuchea and that the Khmer Rouge were being assisted by the Chinese—a relationship agreed upon as early as 1975 by US officials.[76] Such evidence leads to an uncomfortable conclusion: for US decision makers, a Cambodia that had fallen into despotism was preferable to one that had fallen to Vietnamese Communism. Led by Kissinger's "murderous thugs" who were "in many ways worse than Vietnam," the Khmer Rouge would be encouraged clandestinely by a friendly United States and supported by Southeast Asian neighbors in their reorganization of Khmer society. The extermination of Cambodia's population would proceed—without US opposition or condemnation—based on US geopolitical ideology of containment.

CHAPTER 3

Kent State and Cambodia

Reconciliation

Walter Benjamin (1892–1940) was a German-Jewish philosopher and essayist. In the spring of 1940, as he attempted to flee the Nazis, Benjamin wrote, "For every image of the past that is not recognized by the present as one of its own concerns threatens to disappear irretrievably."[1] Benjamin's words are haunting, not only because they evoke memories of the unfolding Holocaust but because they ask us to pause a moment and think about how past events have shaped our present.

Why do we remember the shootings that happened on May 4, 1970? Every year students, faculty, and community members hold a candlelight vigil to remember and honor Allison Krause, Jeffrey Miller, Sandy Scheuer, and William Schroeder. These vigils are cathartic; they provide us a moment to contemplate lives lost and, perhaps, to resolve to prevent similar tragedies from happening in the future. This requires, however, an ability to make sense of the past, to draw meaning from presidential speeches, student protests, and the actions of National Guardsmen—in short, to inquire, learn, and reflect. The vigils allow us to confront the chaos and confusion, the crack of the rifle, and the cry of despair. The memory of May 4 lives on every time someone walks across the campus of Kent State University and wonders, *why did it happen?*

Equally important is to ask, *what of the people of Cambodia?* Simply put, as we grapple with the legacy of the Kent State shootings, we should also grapple with the larger context of the protests: the decision to bomb and invade a neutral country, the violence and genocide that followed. For just as Americans struggle with the violence that transpired on May 4, 1970, the people of Cambodia struggle also with the pain of war, loss, and death.

The act of memorializing is a collective activity. As Barbie Zelizer explains, "Collective memories allow for the fabrication, rearrangement, elaboration, and omission of details about the past, often pushing aside accuracy and authenticity so as to accommodate broader issues of identity formation, power and authority, and political affiliation."[2] There is, in other words, a politics of memory, a recognition that "what is commemorated is not synonymous with what has happened in the past."[3] Indeed, the ability to make sense of the past is fraught with present and future contestations over meaning. What do we say (or not say) about the past? Whose history do we remember? Whose history do we forget? What does the differential treatment of histories tell us about power relations and patterns of inequality within society? Not everything is memorialized, and this makes all the difference in how—and what—we remember.

The contestation over the past finds expression on the landscape. From markers placed over graves to massive monuments to remember certain events, the human landscape is a visible story of our collective past. Memorials help construct memory through their design, which plays a critical role in conveying social and cultural messages; memorials influence how people individually and collectively remember and interpret the past.[4] Across the campus of Kent State University, at least twelve memorials stand in memory of the May 4 shootings. In Cambodia, over eighty memorials commemorate the country's genocide. In this chapter, we explore the memorialization process at Kent State University and in Cambodia and reflect upon the parallel arcs of remembrance of a particular historical moment that unites those who protested Nixon's decision and those who suffered the consequences of that decision.

Remembering May 4, 1970, at Kent State

"It is generally assumed that the social remembering of cultural events is a good thing . . . however, almost every major step in the social remembering processes associated with the May 4, 1970, shootings has been characterized by controversy and debate," writes Jerry Lewis, now a retired KSU faculty member and eyewitness to the May 4 shootings.[5] In 1978, for example, then Kent State president Brage Golding wrote, "Had everyone who has expressed an opinion about the 'meaning of the Kent State tragedy' sent a check for $5, we would have been able to erect a very imposing statue long ago. The trouble is, no group composed of more than one could have agreed on what it should look like. Therefore, we will wait a bit for history to make up its mind."[6] History, however, has not waited and the commemorative landscape at Kent State is as expansive as it is complex, reflecting also that history alone does not make its own meaning. Indeed, since that tragic day in 1970, May 4 observances at Kent State, according to historian John O'Hara, have undergone a marked change, turning from somber, mournful reminders of a violent and troublesome past to sometimes buoyant fetes of postwar unity and historical reconciliation.[7] In this brief section, we reflect upon the myriad traditional rituals and physical memorials that constitute the commemorative field of Kent State. Our purpose is necessarily selective, with an eye toward saying something not principally about the ongoing memorialization of May 4 but instead to look anew at the memorial landscape of Cambodia after Kent State.

The oldest and least controversial rituals in the remembrance of May 4, 1970, are the annual Candlelight March and Vigil. On May 3 at 11:00 P.M. every year since the shooting, participants gather at the Victory Bell for a silent, candlelit march around campus. The marchers weave their way from the Victory Bell, where students gathered on May 4, 1970, to the Prentice parking lot where National Guardsmen killed four students. After the recitation of the Lord's Prayer and the Kaddish, volunteers stand vigil throughout the night while holding commemorative candles in the parking spots where Bill, Jeff, Sandy, and Allison fell.[8]

The vigil concludes shortly after noon on May 4, when the participants march the candles to the stage for the start of the official commemoration. For the first five years, the university planned the event. However, in 1975, KSU decided to distance itself from the annual observance. In that year, the May 4 Task Force, an organization of students, community members, and even some of the students wounded on May 4, assumed primary responsibility for planning the annual noon to 2:00 P.M. commemoration. The program includes a moment of silence at 12:24 P.M., the exact time of the shootings, the ringing of the Victory Bell for the victims of Kent State and Jackson State, a speaker for each of the four fallen students, and a keynote speaker selected by the task force.[9] Out of respect, the university cancels classes for the duration of the program.

At the conclusion of the procession, participants place their lit candles around the B'nai B'rith Hillel marker. On May 4, 1971, the B'nai B'rith Hillel center, with the support of faculty, installed a small plaque with the names of the four fallen students in the place where they fell (now Prentice Hall parking lot). Three of the four students killed were Jewish. In the intervening years, officials have had to replace the plaque. In 1974 vandals stole the plaque just before the commemoration and returned it riddled with bullets; the marker was replaced the following year. Three years later, the plastic frame around the replacement plaque was accidently burned when marchers placed their candles too close to the structure and it was again replaced. Finally, in 1980, to prevent future damage, a deep concrete anchor fixed the marker.[10] Today, one of the damaged markers is on permanent display in the May 4 Resource Room of the Kent State University Library.

Participants gather silently around the B'nai B'rith Hillel marker on May 3, 1975, during the annual commemoration. (Photo by Kent State University's News Service. Courtesy of Kent State University Libraries, Special Collections and Archives.)

For almost twenty years, the B'nai B'rith Hillel marker and a sculpture titled *The Kent Four* by Alastair Jackson stood alone on campus marking the May 4 events. In fact, in 1978 KSU controversially turned down a sculpture by celebrated artist George Segal, as the university deemed it too violent. The work, which is now on display at Princeton University, features a fatherlike figure preparing to kill his son, inspired by the biblical story of Abraham and Isaac. However, in preparation for the twentieth anniversary of the May 4 shootings, the university launched a national memorial design competition. The process progressed smoothly until the university announced the winner but then disqualified him because he was not a US citizen, as required by the contest. Once the university declared the second-place submission by Bruno Ast the winner, the Kent chapter of the American Legion unanimously adopted a resolution opposing the plan to build any type of memorial to what

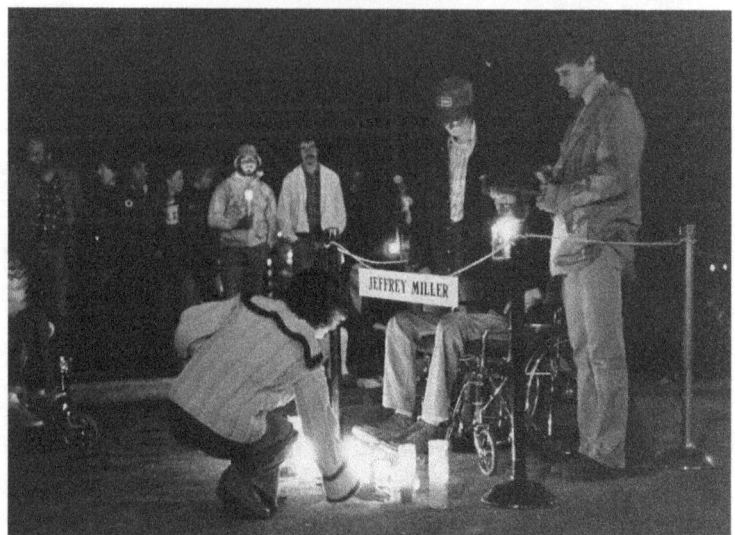

Dean Kahler, one of the students wounded during the shootings, holds a candle on May 3, 1977, at the spot where Jeffrey Miller was killed. (Photo by Kent State University's News Service. Courtesy of Kent State University Libraries, Special Collections and Archives.)

it perceived as student "terrorists." In the end, on May 4, 1990, the university dedicated a significantly scaled-down version of Ast's original design.[11] In response for calls to recognize the wounded students, the larger memorial now includes a plaque with their names alongside those of the four fallen students. On the memorial are the words "Inquire. Learn. Reflect." Notably, in one of the few references to the political context of the protests, students planted 58,175 daffodils in the hill next to the memorial. Professor Brinsley Tyrrell suggested the addition, with each daffodil representing a soldier who had died in Vietnam, thus connecting the lives lost on campus to the Americans lost in the war.[12]

In contrast to the large committee behind the memorial selection process, a relatively small but powerful group of the victims' family members and the May 4 Task Force successfully lobbied university president Carol Cartwright to create memorials that mark the approximate locations of where Sandy, Bill, Jeff, and Allison fell on May 4, 1970. On May 4, 1998, the May 4 Task Force staged a walkover to the president's office to demand that the university heed the wishes of the family members by creating memorials for their loved ones in the Prentice Hall parking lot. The Office of the University Architect designed the markers and the university dedicated the site on September 8, 1999, purposely before the annual commemoration to allow for a more private ceremony.[13]

In 2006 an Ohio Historical Society marker was erected with a short description of the events and in 2010, the May 4 Walking Tour, consisting of seven interpretative trail markers with associated short documentaries, was created to add context and depth to the memorial landscape. The May 4 Visitors Center was opened on campus two years later. The center houses a permanent exhibit on the history and legacy of May 4, 1970, as well as temporary

A sizable crowd braves the rain for the dedication of the May 4 Memorial on May 4, 1990. (Courtesy of Kent State University Libraries, Special Collections and Archives.)

exhibit spaces and a room to accommodate tours and programming. It serves as a gateway to the more expansive site that was officially declared a National Historic Landmark in 2016.

When Ohio National Guardsmen shot at a crowd of Kent State students who were protesting Nixon's expansion of the Vietnam War into Cambodia, the subsequent deaths of Allison Krause, Jeffrey Miller, Sandy Scheuer, and William Schroeder forever altered the university. Over time, the Kent State community has created an expansive, albeit contested, memorial landscape in an effort both to mourn and to provide meaning.[14] We believe that it is necessary, in the spirit of the antiwar protesters, to remain vigilant to their concerns and to keep foremost in our minds the legacy that Nixon's decision had both on American society and on the people of Cambodia who endured years of armed conflict and genocide. To this end, we now reflect upon efforts to remember Cambodia after Kent State.

Remembering Cambodia after Kent State

Decades after the cessation of direct violence, the question of reconciliation in Cambodia remains fraught, in part because of competing claims over the meaning of reconciliation but also because of the authorship of Cambodia's past.[15] In Cambodia, approximately eighty local memorials dot the landscape, each an intimate expression of grief and suffering, but also hope.[16] Most foreigners to Cambodia, however, will not see these local memorials; nor will they witness the hauntingly beautiful rituals of reverence and remembrance. The vast majority of international tourists form their understanding of the legacy of the Khmer Rouge era around the Tuol Sleng Genocide Museum and the Choeung Ek Genocidal Center. Located in Phnom Penh, Tuol Sleng had once been a high school. During the genocide, the Khmer Rouge converted the buildings into a "security center," one of more than two hundred such centers located throughout the country. Throughout its brief existence, Khmer Rouge cadre arrested, detained, and tortured approximately eighteen thousand men, women, and children; all but a handful were executed. Some killings took place at Tuol Sleng, although most occurred outside of Phnom Penh, at a Chinese cemetery known as Choeung Ek.[17]

Monuments, memorials, and museums are important symbolic sites, and the history of their formation greatly informs how we remember and understand the past. In this section, we reflect upon the official "meaning making" of the Cambodian genocide as commemorated at the Tuol Sleng Genocide Museum and the Choeung Ek Genocidal Center. Together, these two sites offer an opportunity to think about the memorialization of the genocide but, equally important, how these memories are (and continue to be) shaped for political purposes.

On December 25, 1978, Vietnamese forces totaling more than a hundred thousand troops joined with approximately twenty thousand former Khmer Rouge cadre and surged into Democratic Kampuchea. Within weeks, the Khmer Rouge regime was overthrown, ending the Cambodian genocide. Vietnamese authorities installed a new government and renamed Cambodia as the People's Republic of Kampuchea (PRK). For millions of men, women, and children, the terror of genocide was over, but the suffering remained. Cambodia was a broken country; famine and disease hung as specters over the land. Survivors wandered from village to village, seeking lost relatives and friends.

The military defeat of the Khmer Rouge ushered in a new period for Cambodia—a decade of Vietnamese occupation and sporadic guerrilla fighting with the still-active Khmer Rouge. According to David Chandler, the fledging People's Republic of Kampuchea and its Vietnamese advisers faced enormous economic, organizational, and social problems. An international community that by and large condemned Vietnam's liberation of Cambodia as an "invasion" compounded problems. In the United States, for example, the presidential administration of Jimmy Carter supported the exiled

Khmer Rouge as the rightful government. In the aftermath of its devastating loss in Indochina, the United States was intolerant of Vietnam and remained in steadfast opposition to the newly installed People's Republic of Kampuchea.

The political context of the People's Republic of Kampuchea significantly informs the memorialization of the Cambodian genocide. Simply put, representatives both of Vietnam and the People's Republic of Kampuchea had to defend their military overthrow of the previous regime. They did so by correctly identifying Khmer Rouge practice as genocidal. In 1979, however, neither the United Nations nor several key countries, including the United States and China, agreed that genocide had taken place. Adding to the difficulties was the fact that the new government was largely composed of former Khmer Rouge cadre. This fact alone negated any type of victor's justice as it was impossible to place blame exclusively on the former regime without calling into question one's own involvement and investment. Furthermore, to the outside world, it appeared as if one Communist country, Vietnam, overthrew another Communist country, Democratic Kampuchea. It was not possible to place the blame on Communist ideology. Such was the context for the creation of the Tuol Sleng Museum of Genocide.

The act of remembering was swift in the making. In the days following the defeat of the Khmer Rouge, two Vietnamese photojournalists were walking through the deserted streets of Phnom Penh. On one day, the stench of decomposing bodies drew them to a walled compound. Upon entering, the photojournalists found the bodies of several recently murdered men. Indeed, some remained chained to iron beds where they had been tortured. Over the next several days, Vietnamese officials and their Cambodian assistants searched the former school and recovered thousands of documents: mug shots and undeveloped negatives, thousands of written confessions, hundreds of cadre notebooks, numerous DK publications, and myriad instruments of torture and detainment.[18]

The compound discovered by the photojournalists was the site of the infamous security center used by the Khmer Rouge and leadership of the People's Republic of Kampuchea, and the Vietnamese recognized immediately that the compound provided a political opportunity. As Rachel Hughes explains, the long-term national and international legitimacy of the People's Republic of Kampuchea hinged on the exposure of the violent excesses of Pol Pot and the continued production of a coherent memory of the past—that is, of liberation and reconstruction at the hands of a benevolent fraternal state.[19] The task fell to Mai Lam, a Vietnamese colonel who had extensive experience in legal studies and museology. Drawing inspiration from the many Holocaust memorials he visited, Mai Lam styled the Tuol Sleng Genocide Museum as an "Asian Auschwitz." So quick was the rush to memorialize the genocide for political

Memorial stupa at the Tuol Sleng Genocide Museum. (Courtesy of James A. Tyner.)

purposes that on January 25, 1979, less than three weeks after the downfall of the Khmer Rouge, the museum was visited by a group of journalists invited precisely to spread word of the crimes of Pol Pot and his henchman, Ieng Sary. The museum opened to the public in July 1980.

Mai Lam largely retained the structures at Tuol Sleng, with only minor modifications made to the site. Surrounded by a corrugated tin fence topped with coils of barbed wire, Tuol Sleng consists of four three-story concrete buildings arranged in a U-shaped pattern around a grassy courtyard dotted with palm trees. In the middle is the former administrative building. To the south of the courtyard, Mai Lam installed fourteen tombstones, in remembrance of the fourteen men and boys thought to have survived their imprisonment at S-21. The actual number of people who survived incarceration remains contested.

Visitors to Tuol Sleng are directed first to Building A, located at the southern end of the compound. Here, Khmer Rouge cadre converted the former schoolrooms into makeshift torture chambers. Now, rooms are empty, save for the rusty metal beds, shackles, and various instruments of torture. Grainy photographs of corpses discovered in January 1979 hang mutely on the wall. Until 2010, blood from the victims stained the floors. Adjoining Building A are two buildings that were used to detain prisoners. Building B consists of communal holding cells. Now thousands of black-and-white photographs taken of the unnamed prisoners upon their entry to Tuol Sleng fill the vacuous rooms. The Khmer Rouge also detained prisoners in Building C. However, in this building prison guards converted the former classrooms into several individual cells for important prisoners. Directly opposite Building A, on the northern end of the compound, sits Building D. The Khmer Rouge also detained prisoners here; it now houses various instruments of torture, thousands of shackles, and disinterred skulls.

The display of physical horrors—the shackles, instruments of torture, and human skulls—serves not any reconciliation purpose but instead political goals: the legitimacy of political rule in the country.[20] As David Chandler explains, "Mai Lam wanted to arrange Cambodia's recent past to fit the requirements of the PRK and its Vietnamese mentors as well as the long-term needs, as he saw them, of the Cambodian people."[21] The former would take precedence over the latter. Indeed, according to Bridgett Sion, the "rush to turn a death site into a gallery for visitors is [an] indication that the new leadership had less concern about the memory of victims than about using the site for immediate political purposes."[22]

Memorial exhibits at S-21 are graphic and poignant. Visitors walk freely within the former prison cells and, until recently, touched the rusty shackles that once detained thousands of men, women, and children destined to die. Visitors gaze at row upon row of photographs of people long since dead, but there is little to indicate who they were or why they died. Few photographs include names. Overall, the purpose of the museum is not to explain the events that led to genocide, as the wider dimensions of the Cold War and armed conflict in Indochina remain vague.

Notably, the political decisions of foreign actors, including those of Nixon and Kissinger, go unmentioned. Instead, the names of only a few senior leaders of Khmer Rouge cadre appear throughout the museum, namely Pol Pot, Ieng Sary, Nuon Chea, and Khieu Samphan. Likewise, museum displays portray their actions as isolated events, for example, with scant reference to the assistance provided by the Vietnamese Communist Party in achieving power. Rather than directly addressing the complicated past, the new regime promoted a selective remembrance, but not a reconciliation or an account of the past.

The killing grounds at Choeung Ek have also been memorialized. In 1988 the government opened the site to the public. Following a mass exhumation around 1980, a central stupa filled with skeletal remains was erected, and many simple wooden structures marking the location of burial pits were constructed. Early on, the few visitors who journeyed to Choeung Ek arrived via a dirt road. There was no formal entrance to the site, as there were no walls demarcating the boundaries of the cemetery. A solitary gift shop sat off to the side. In 2005, however, a Japanese company obtained from the Cambodian government a thirty-year license to operate the site. Now visitors, most of whom are foreigners, experience anything

Memorial stupa at the Choeung Ek Genocidal Center. (Courtesy of James A. Tyner.)

Craters from the US bombing campaign remain visible on the Cambodian landscape today. (Courtesy of James A. Tyner.)

but an authentic burial site. Where once a dirt road buttressed by rice fields brought the few visitors to the site, now they arrive via a tarmac road, lined with bars, cafés, hotels, and football pitches. A faded sign advertises a nearby shooting range where, for a small fee, guests can fire automatic weapons and even grenade launchers. Upon entering the cemetery through an elaborate gated entrance, visitors line up at a ticket counter before proceeding on to an audio-assisted walking tour. Public toilets, a snack shop, and a renovated gift shop—periodically selling replica Khmer Rouge clothing—cater to the needs of visitors who listen to an abbreviated history of Chocung Ek and the genocide. An air-conditioned screening room also shows a brief documentary of the genocide.

Tuol Sleng is but one of hundreds of security centers, and Choeung Ek is but one of thousands of killing fields throughout Cambodia. The privileging of these two sites as the official bearers of memory thus belies a landscape of active memorialization. As such, the preservation of local memorials, away from the gaze of foreign tourists, offers insight into the fragmented collective memories that circulate throughout the country. Indeed, away from the authorized state narratives promoted at iconic sites such as the Tuol Sleng Genocide Museum and the graves at Choeung Ek, throughout Cambodia many villagers "collectively put in place new practices of remembrance."[23] Anne Guillou explains that while "bushes and forests were progressively cleared, roads were built, and rice and fruit trees were planted over the mass graves," these sites are remembered daily by the survivors, for the "peasants remember each pond, well, and field where bodies were found."[24]

Those who lived through the Pol Pot regime, the Cambodia after the Kent State shootings, speak of a disconnect between the official narrative of genocide and their lived reality of violence, a reality that they relive daily as they use the dams, reservoirs, and roads constructed during the Khmer Rouge years. These men and women speak often out of a need not to forget as opposed to an obligation to remember. We should heed their efforts, for it remains our responsibility to carry forward the spirit of those who protested at Kent State on May 4, 1970, and their hope to make the world more peaceful.

Notes

1. The Path to May 4

1. Thomas M. Grace, *Kent State: Dissent in the Long Sixties* (Amherst: Univ. of Massachusetts Press, 2016), 22–23.

2. Grace, *Kent State*, 24.

3. Grace, *Kent State*, 62.

4. "Now It's Official! No Hours for Girls This Fall," *Daily Kent Stater,* Apr. 4, 1969, https://dks.library.kent.edu/?a=d&d=dks19690404-01.2.7 &srpos=27& e=-------en-20--21-byDA-txt-txIN-+No+Hours+for+Girls+ this+Fall------.

5. Grace, *Kent State*, 137–39.

6. Grace, *Kent State*, 142–43.

7. For more information on BUS and black student activism at Kent State University, see Lae'l Hughes Watkins, "Between Two Worlds: A Look at the Impact of the Black Campus Movement on the Antiwar Era of 1968–1970 at Kent State University," *Ohio History* 124, no. 1 (Spring 2017): 41–64.

8. For more on this debate, see Mark Atwood Lawrence, *The Vietnam War: A Concise International History* (New York City: Oxford Univ. Press, 2008), 1–16.

9. For example, see Mark Kurlansky, *1968: The Year That Rocked the World* (New York: Random House Publishing, 2005).

10. For more information on Nixon's "Silent Majority" speech, see Sarah Thelen, "Mobilizing a Majority: Nixon's 'Silent Majority' Speech and the Domestic Debate over Vietnam," *Journal of American Studies* 51, no. 2 (Aug. 2017): 887–914, https://doi.org/10.1017/S0021875816001936.

11. John A. Farrell, *Richard Nixon: A Life* (New York: Doubleday, 2017), 342–43.

12. For more information on the Chennault Affair, see Ken Hughes, *Chasing Shadows: The Nixon Tapes, the Chennault Affair, and the Origins of Watergate* (Charlottesville: Univ. of Virginia Press, 2015).

13. Robert Dallek, *Nixon and Kissinger: Partners in Power* (New York: Harper Collins Publisher, 2007), 117.

14. Walter Isaacson, *Kissinger: A Biography* (New York: Simon and Schuster Paperbacks, 2005), 171.

15. Isaacson, *Kissinger,* 172.

16. Dallek, *Nixon and Kissinger,* 119.

17. Richard Reeves, *President Nixon: Alone in the White House* (New York: Simon and Schuster, 2001), 58–59.

18. Reeves, *President Nixon,* 59.

19. "Memorandum from the President's Assistant for National Security Affairs (Kissinger) to President Nixon," Office of the Historian, https://history.state.gov/historicaldocuments/frus1969-76v06/d52, accessed Nov. 20, 2018.

20. Richard M. Nixon, *Public Papers of the Presidents of the United States,* Washington, DC, Office of the Federal Register, National Archives and Records Administration (US GPO, 1971), 547–57.

21. "Hear Us," *Daily Kent Stater,* Oct. 15, 1969, https://dks.library.kent.edu/?a=d&d=dks19691015-01.2.6&srpos=9& e=-------en-20--1-byDA-txt -txIN-moratorium+march------.

22. Amy J. Rutenburg, "How the Draft Reshaped America," *New York Times,* Oct. 6, 2017, https://www.nytimes.com/2017/10/06/opinion/vietnam-draft.html.

23. Lawrence, *Vietnam War,* 148.

24. Grace, *Kent State,* 199.

25. Juan De Onus, "Nixon Puts 'Bum' Label on Some College Radicals," *New York Times,* May 2, 1970, https://www.nytimes.com/1970/05/02/archives/nixon-puts-bums-label-on-some-college-radicals-nixon-denounces-bums.html.

26. Grace, *Kent State,* 200–202.

27. Carole A. Barbato, Laura L. Davis, and Mark F. Seeman, *This We Know: A Chronology of the Shootings at Kent State, May 1970* (Kent, OH: Kent State Univ. Press, 2012), 6.

28. Craig S. Simpson and Gregory S. Wilson, *Above the Shots: An Oral History of the Kent State Shootings* (Kent, OH: Kent State Univ. Press, 2016), 71.

29. To quote Barbato, Davis, and Seeman, "Although it is widely assumed that the building was burned by demonstrators, it has also been suggested

by some researchers that the arson was the work of agents provocateurs" (*This We Know*, 7).

30. Barbato, Davis, and Seeman, *This We Know*, 71–72.

31. James A. Rhodes, "Speech on Campus Disorders in Kent," May 3, 1970, https://www.library.kent.edu/ksu-may-4-rhodes-speech-may-3-1970, accessed Nov. 21, 2018.

32. Howard Means, *67 Shots: Kent State and End of American Innocence* (Philadelphia: Da Capo Press, 2016), 56–58.

33. Grace, *Kent State*, 211.

34. Barbato, Davis, and Seeman, *This We Know*, 15–17.

35. Barbato, Davis, and Seeman, *This We Know*, 19–21.

36. Professors Thomas R. Hensley and Jerry M. Lewis give an excellent summary of this debate in "The May 4 Shootings at Kent State University: The Search for Historical Accuracy," in *Kent State and May 4th: A Social Science Perspective* (Kent, OH: Kent State Univ. Press, 2010), 54–60. In years of court cases, the Guard argued that they fired because they feared for their lives. Many scholars challenge this claim of self-defense. Some argue that members of the Guard huddled in the practice football field and conspired to shoot at the students. Others believe that audio evidence, which only emerged in 2007, conclusively proves that there was a clear order to fire. Still, others find the evidence inconclusive but agree with the Scranton Commission on Campus Unrest, which concluded that the firing was "unnecessary, unwarranted, and inexcusable."

2. Cambodia after May 4

1. Michael Vickery, "How Many Died in Pol Pot's Kampuchea?," *Bulletin of Concerned Asian Scholars* 20 (1988): 377–85; Ben Kiernan, "The Genocide in Cambodia, 1975–1979," *Bulletin of Concerned Asian Scholars* 22 (1990): 35–40; Patrick Heuveline, "'Between One and Three Million': Towards the Demographic Reconstruction of a Decade of Cambodian History (1970–1979)," *Population Studies* 52 (1998): 49–65; Damien de Walque, "Selective Mortality during the Khmer Rouge Period in Cambodia," *Population and Development Review* 31 (2005): 351–68; Damien de Walque, "The Socio-Demographic Legacy of the Khmer Rouge Period in Cambodia," *Population Studies* 60 (2006): 223–31.

2. The total number of deaths attributed to the genocide is subject to debate. Estimates range from 1.5 million to upwards of 3 million deaths. Also problematic is the attribution of deaths to the genocidal per se, that is, the years between 1975 and 1979, and the preceding period of US

bombing (1968–73) and subsequent civil war (1970–75). See, for example, Vickery, "How Many Died in Pol Pot's Kampuchea?"; Heuveline, "Between One and Three Million"; and de Walque "Selective Mortality during the Khmer Rouge Period."

3. Ben Kiernan, *How Pol Pot Came to Power: A History of Communism in Kampuchea, 1930–1975* (London: Verso, 1985), xx.

4. Jonathan Neale, *A People's History of the Vietnam War* (New York: New Press, 2003), 33.

5. Gareth Porter, "Vietnamese Communist Policy toward Kampuchea, 1930–1970," in *Revolution and Its Aftermath: Eight Essays,* ed. David P. Chandler and Ben Kiernan (New Haven, CT: Yale Univ. Southeast Asia Studies, 1983), 73.

6. Johan van de Ven, "Without an End in Sight: Competition between the People's Republic of China and the Soviet Union during the Vietnam War and Its Implications for the Wider Relationship," *Asiadémica: Revista Universitaria de Estudios Sobre Asia Oriental* 5 (2015): 50–51.

7. van de Ven, "Without an End in Sight," 53; Jian Chen and Kuisong Yang, "Chinese Politics and the Collapse of the Sino-Soviet Alliance," in *Brothers in Arms: The Rise and Fall of the Sino-Soviet Alliance, 1945–1963,* ed. Odd Arne Westad (Washington, DC: Woodrow Wilson Center Press, 1998), 276.

8. van de Ven, "Without an End in Sight," 56.

9. van de Ven, "Without an End in Sight," 56.

10. Kiernan, *How Pol Pot Came to Power,* xx.

11. Steve Heder, *Cambodian Communism and the Vietnamese Model: Imitation and Independence, 1930–1975* (Bangkok: White Lotus Press, 2004), 93.

12. Margaret Slocomb, *The People's Republic of Kampuchea, 1979–1989: The Revolution after Pol Pot* (Chiang Mai, Thailand: Silkworm Books, 2003), 10.

13. Heder, *Cambodian Communism,* 11.

14. Slocomb, *The People's Republic of Kampuchea,* 11.

15. Ben Kiernan and Taylor Owen, "Roots of U.S. Troubles in Afghanistan: Civilian Bombing Casualties and the Cambodian Precedent," *Asia-Pacific Journal* 8, no. 26 (June 28, 2010): 7.

16. Kenton Clymer, *Troubled Relations: The United States and Cambodia since 1870* (DeKalb: Northern Illinois Univ. Press, 2007), 137.

17. Operation Menu comprised six bombing campaigns, known as Breakfast, Lunch, Snack, Supper, Dinner, and Dessert. Each campaign targeted a specific base area located in Cambodia. See Ben Kiernan, "The American Bombardment of Kampuchea, 1969–1973," *Vietnam Generation* 1, no. 1 (1989): 4–14; William Shawcross, *Sideshow: Kissinger, Nixon, and the Destruction of Cambodia,* rev. ed. (New York: Cooper Square Press, 2002); Taylor Owen and Ben Kiernan, "Bombs over Cambodia," *Walrus*

Magazine (Oct. 2006): 62–69; and Ben Kiernan and Taylor Owen, "Making More Enemies than We Kill? Calculating U.S. Bomb Tonnages Dropped on Laos and Cambodia, and Weighing Their Implications," *Asia-Pacific Journal* 13, no. 16 (2015): 1–9.

18. As indicated, several covert missions had been under way in Cambodia since at least 1965.

19. Qtd. in Wilfred P. Deac, *Road to the Killing Fields: The Cambodian War of 1970–1975* (College Station: Texas A&M Univ. Press, 1997), 77.

20. Richard M. Nixon, "Address to the Nation on the Situation in Southeast Asia," Apr. 30, 1970, www.nixonlibrary.org, accessed Oct. 6, 2019.

21. Qtd. in Shawcross, *Sideshow*, 145.

22. Qtd. in Shawcross, *Sideshow*, 145.

23. Bernard K. Gordon and Kathryn Young, "The Khmer Republic: That Was the Cambodia That Was," *Asian Survey* 11, no. 1 (1971): 27.

24. Qtd. in Kiernan and Owen, "Roots of U.S. Troubles."

25. Kiernan and Owen, "Roots of U.S. Troubles"; see also Shawcross, *Sideshow*, 145.

26. Qtd. in Kiernan and Owen, "Roots of U.S. Troubles."

27. Kiernan and Owen, "Roots of U.S. Troubles." Kiernan and Owen reveal that between 1965 and 1973 approximately five hundred thousand tons of US bombs were dropped on Cambodia; this total surpasses the tonnage that US forces dropped in the Pacific theater during World War II and in the Korean War. On a per capita basis, the bombing exceeded the total Allied bombing of Germany and Japan.

28. Shawcross, *Sideshow*, 294–95.

29. John Tully, *A Short History of Cambodia: From Empire to Survival* (Crow's Nest, Australia: Allen and Unwin, 2005), 167.

30. Qtd. in Kiernan, *Pol Pot Regime*, 22.

31. Shawcross, *Sideshow*, 122; Clymer, *Troubled Relations*, 102.

32. Lien-Hang T. Nguyen, *Hanoi's War: An International History of the War for Peace in Vietnam* (Chapel Hill: Univ. of North Carolina Press, 2012), 170.

33. Nguyen, *Hanoi's War*, 170.

34. Nhem, *The Khmer Rouge*, 22. In reality, Pol Pot assumed control of all military activity.

35. Qtd. in Kiernan, "American Bombardment," 9.

36. Qtd. in Kiernan, "American Bombardment," 9.

37. Clymer, *Troubled Relations*, 119.

38. Arnold R. Isaacs, *Without Honor: Defeat in Cambodia* (Baltimore: Johns Hopkins Univ. Press, 1983), 199. See also Noam Chomsky and Edward S. Herman, *After the Cataclysm: Postwar Indochina and the Reconstruction of Imperial Ideology* (Chicago: Haymarket Books, 2014).

39. Isaacs, *Without Honor,* 209.

40. Isaacs, *Without Honor,* 224.

41. Internal factions among the CPK leadership would result in widespread purges.

42. James A. Tyner, *From Rice Fields to Killing Fields: Nature, Life, and Labor under the Khmer Rouge* (Syracuse, NY: Syracuse Univ. Press, 2017).

43. Alexander L. Hinton, *Why Did They Kill? Cambodia in the Shadow of Genocide* (Berkeley: Univ. of California Press, 2005), 48.

44. Document D30882, "Long Live the 17th Anniversary of the Communist Party of Kampuchea," Documentation Center of Cambodia, Phnom Penh.

45. Document D30882, "Long Live the 17th Anniversary."

46. Ben Kiernan, "Khmer Rouge Biographical Questionnaire," Yale University Genocide Studies Program, http://gsp.yale.edu/khmer-rouge-biographical-questionnaire, accessed Oct. 6, 2019.

47. Ben Kiernan, *The Pol Pot Regime: Race, Power, and Genocide in Cambodia under the Khmer Rouge, 1975–79* (New Haven, CT: Yale Univ. Press, 1996).

48. Document D30882, "Long Live the 17th Anniversary."

49. Document D30882, "Long Live the 17th Anniversary."

50. It remains unclear if the senior leadership of the CPK even intended for the workers to assume decision-making capabilities, as theorized in democratic centralism, or if this was a ruse from the outset.

51. Communist Party of Kampuchea (CPK), "Four-Year Plan," in *Pol Pot Plans the Future: Confidential Leadership Documents from Democratic Kampuchea, 1976–1977,* ed. David Chandler, Ben Kiernan, and Chanthou Boua (New Haven, CT: Yale Univ. Southeast Asia Studies, 1988), 51.

52. Michael P. Todaro, *Economic Development in the Third World,* 4th ed. (New York: Longman, 1989), 428.

53. Document D00698, "Cooperation with the Ministry of Commerce," Documentation Center of Cambodia, Phnom Penh.

54. Document D00698, "Cooperation with the Ministry of Commerce."

55. CPK, "Report of Activities of the Party Center According to the General Political Tasks of 1976," in Chandler, Kiernan, and Boua, *Pol Pot Plans the Future,* 200.

56. CPK, "Report of Activities," 200.

57. CPK, "Preliminary Explanation before Reading the Plan, by the Party Secretary," in Chandler, Kiernan, and Boua, *Pol Pot Plans the Future,* 131.

58. CPK, "Four-Year Plan," 51.

59. CPK, "Four-Year Plan," 89.

60. CPK, "Four-Year Plan," 89.

61. James A. Tyner et al., "Khmer Rouge Irrigation Schemes during the Cambodian Genocide," *Genocide Studies International* 12, no. 1 (2018): 103–19.

62. Kalyanee Mam, "The Endurance of the Cambodian Family under the Khmer Rouge Regime: An Oral History," in *Genocide in Cambodia and Rwanda: New Perspectives*, ed. Susan E. Cook (New Haven, CT: Yale Center for International and Area Studies, 2004), 134–35.

63. Document D30882, "Long Live the 17th Anniversary."

64. Document D30882, "Long Live the 17th Anniversary."

65. Document D30882, "Long Live the 17th Anniversary."

66. Memorandum of Conversation, "Secretary's Meeting with Foreign Minister Chatchai of Thailand," Nov. 26, 1975, http://nsarchive.gwu/NSAEBB /NSAEBB198, accessed Feb. 15, 2016. Others in attendance included US deputy secretary Robert Ingersoll and Brent Scowcroft, member of the National Security Council.

67. Kissinger is referring to the evacuation of Phnom Penh whereby millions of people were forced at gunpoint to relocate to agricultural collectives throughout the country. This forced removal is part of the prosecution's case on crimes against humanity and genocide at the Khmer Rouge Tribunal.

68. Chatchai's question refers to the dominant narrative of the "domino theory."

69. Andrew Mertha, *Brothers in Arms: Chinese Aid to the Khmer Rouge, 1975–1979* (Ithaca, NY: Cornell Univ. Press, 2014).

70. "Embassy Jakarta Telegram 1579 to Secretary State, 6 December 1975," National Security Archive, http://nsarchive.gwu.edu/NSAEBB/NSA EBB62/doc4.pdf, accessed Feb. 23, 2016.

71. It is striking that Suharto stated matter-of-factly that the Khmer Rouge leadership was "closer to Hanoi." In this instance, Suharto ascribed considerably more authority and influence to Sihanouk than actually existed.

72. Clymer, *Trouble Relations*, 165n31.

73. Bangkok Embassy Telegram 21997, "Cambodia—Conversations with the Resistance," Sept. 29, 1977, http://nsarchive.gwu/NSAEBB/ NSAEBB463, accessed Feb. 15, 2016.

74. Bangkok Embassy Telegram 21997.

75. Bangkok Embassy Telegram 21997.

76. It is noteworthy that the telegram indicated that Cambodian resistance fighters were "reminded explicitly that the U.S. Government could not . . . become involved in theirs or other internal struggles, nor could the U.S. supply support for their cause."

3. Kent State and Cambodia

1. Walter Benjamin, *Illuminations: Essays and Reflections,* ed. Hannah Arendt (New York: Schocken Books, 1968), 255.

2. Barbie Zelizer, *Remembering to Forget: Holocaust Memory through the Camera's Eye* (Chicago: Univ. of Chicago Press, 1998), 3.

3. Owen J. Dwyer and Derek H. Alderman, "Memorial Landscapes: Analytic Questions and Metaphors," *GeoJournal* 73 (2008): 167.

4. Dwyer and Alderman, "Memorial Landscapes," 167; Christina R. Steidl, "Remembering May 4, 1970: Integrating the Commemorative Field at Kent State," *American Sociological Review* 78, no. 5 (2013): 751.

5. Jerry M. Lewis, "Social Remembering and Kent State," in *Democratic Narrative, History, and Memory,* ed. Carole A. Barbato and Laura L. Davis (Kent, OH: Kent State Univ. Press, 2012), 176.

6. Brage Golding to Gregory P. Torre, Oct. 27, 1978, box 85B, folder 12, May 4 Collection, Special Collections and Archives, Kent State University Libraries, Kent, OH.

7. John Fitzgerald O'Hara, "Kent State/May 4 and Postwar Memory," *American Quarterly* 58 (2006): 301.

8. For more on the candlelight walk and vigil, see Jerry M. Lewis, "The Candlelight Walk and Vigil," in *Kent State and May 4th: A Social Science Perspective,* ed. Thomas R. Hensley and Jerry M. Lewis (Kent, OH: Kent State Univ. Press, 2010), 213–16.

9. On March 6, 2019, the Kent State Board of Trustees passed a resolution affirming "that for the continuity and sustainability of [the May 4 Task Force's] efforts, the time is right for the university to assume responsibility for the annual May 4 commemoration and ongoing educational events through the Office of the President, beginning with the 50th commemoration in 2019–2010." See Madison MacArthur, "Trustees Pass May 4 Resolution: The University Will Assume 50th Commemoration Despite Open Letter from the May 4 Task Force," *Kent Wired,* Mar. 14, 2019, http://www.kentwired.com/latest_updates/article_a2485f82-4071-11e9-bc20-d7264bbcd27b.html.

10. Chris W. Post, "Beyond Kent State? May 4 and Commemorating Violence in Public Space," *Geoforum* 76 (2016): 142–52.

11. Stanford W. Gregory Jr. and Jerry M. Lewis, "Symbols of Collective Memory: The Social Process of Memorializing May 4, 1970, at Kent State University," in *Kent State and May 4th: A Social Science Perspective,* ed. Thomas R. Hensley and Jerry M. Lewis (Kent, OH: Kent State Univ. Press, 2010), 204–5.

12. Steidl, "Remembering May 4, 1970," 761.

13. Post, "Beyond Kent State?," 146.

14. Post, "Beyond Kent State?," 143.

15. Peter Manning, "Reconciliation and Perpetrator Memories in Cambodia," *International Journal of Transitional Justice* 9, no. 3 (2015): 388. For a comprehensive overview of memorial landscapes in Cambodia, see James A. Tyner, *Landscape, Memory, and Post-Violence in Cambodia* (Lanham, MD: Rowman and Littlefield, 2017).

16. See, for example, Caroline Bennett, "Living with the Dead in the Killing Fields of Cambodia," *Journal of Southeast Asian Studies* 49, no. 2 (2018): 184–203.

17. David Chandler, *Voices from S-21: Terror and History in Pol Pot's Secret Prison* (Berkeley: Univ. of California Press, 1999); James A. Tyner, *The Politics of Lists: Bureaucracy and Genocide under the Khmer Rouge* (Morgantown: West Virginia Univ. Press, 2018).

18. Chandler, *Voices from S-21*, 3. See also Tyner, *The Politics of Lists*.

19. Rachel Hughes, "The Abject Artifacts of Memory: Photographs from Cambodia's Genocide," *Media, Culture Society* 25 (2003): 26.

20. Bridgette Sion, "Conflicting Sites of Memory in Post-Genocide Cambodia," *Humanity: An International Journal of Human Rights, Humanitarianism, and Development* 2 (2011): 1–21.

21. Chandler, *Voices from S-21*, 5.

22. Sion, "Conflicting Sites," 5.

23. Anne Yvonne Guillou, "The Living Archaeology of a Painful Heritage: The First and Second Life of the Khmer Rouge Mass Graves," in *"Archaeologizing" Heritage?: Transcultural Entanglements between Local Social Practices and Global Virtual Realities*, ed. M. Falser and J. Juneja (Berlin: Springer-Verlag, 2013), 267.

24. Guillou, "The Living Archaeology," 268.